THE SCHOOLBOY
AND THE SIGNALMAN

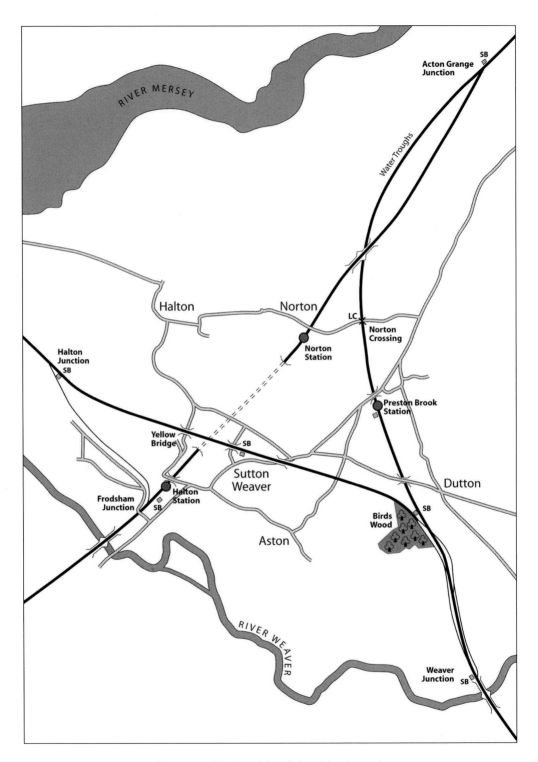

Lines around Birdswood (just below right of centre)

THE SCHOOLBOY AND THE SIGNALMAN

Recollections of Birdswood signal box in the 1950s

PETER HADDOCK

· RAILWAY HERITAGE ·

from

The NOSTALGIA Collection

First published in 2008

British Library Cataloguing in Publication Data

A catalogue record for this book is available from the British Library.

ISBN 978 1 85794 313 9

Silver Link Publishing Ltd
The Trundle
Ringstead Road
Great Addington
Kettering
Northants NN14 4BW

Tel/Fax: 01536 330588
email: sales@nostalgiacollection.com
Website: www.nostalgiacollection.com

Printed and bound in the Czech Republic

Photographed on Saturday 24 April 1954 from alongside the down Liverpool line looking in the down direction, this view shows Britain's first ever flyover (completed in April 1869 by the LNWR), built to carry the up Liverpool track over the West Coast Main line. The strategic position of Birdswood signal box is readily apparent. The tall repeater signal on the lattice post indicates that a train bound for Liverpool is due – the actual Home signal is hidden behind the bushes beyond the man. Some idea of the gradients here can be gained from this picture, as the up and down main lines, both level at this point, run beneath the flyover carrying the up Liverpool line on a falling gradient of 1 in 415. The track in the foreground is climbing at 1 in 151 here, increasing to 1 in 115 before reaching the same level as the up track nearer to Sutton Weaver. Has the smoky chimney of the platelayers hut been cured with a length of metal duct? *C. M. & J. M. Bentley*

CONTENTS

ACKNOWLEDGEMENTS

It would be almost impossible to write a book based upon fact – even though much of it is a recollection of one's own personal experiences – without the generous contributions of many other people, some of whom are very close friends, while others were completely unknown to me. Their knowledge and experience have been written into this book, either directly or in a way that has helped form a foundation upon which these chapters have been built. It is therefore with grateful appreciation that I acknowledge the valuable input of the following people.

First of all my very good friend John Hillier, whose own thorough researches into the railways around Cheadle Heath, Stockport, presented in a most interesting and attractive manner, inspired me with the idea of gathering together as much information as possible about the signal box at Birdswood and the area it controlled.

Next, the kind Editor of *Rail News* who, in February 1996, converted my brief letter requesting information about Birdswood signal box from anyone who remembered it into an interesting small feature article. As a result of this, Trevor Booth of Cuddington, Cheshire, a signalling technician, responded with three photographs of the signal box and much other very useful information.

Reg Instone of the Signalling Record Society, together with colleagues, provided me with maps, track diagrams and other information, and stimulated my own personal recollections of Birdswood.

The late Jim Peden of Liverpool tirelessly searched his photographic archives to provide some pictures of trains and installations in the area. More than this, he went to great lengths to properly interpret my rather finicky instructions for enlargements and followed them to the letter with, I believe you will agree, excellent results.

Much kindly help was received from a life-long railwayman, Michael Bentley of Buxton, who found among his many thousands of negatives some excellent views of Birdswood box and surrounding area. An accomplished railway author himself, Michael gave me much useful and kindly advice.

Ray Miller, of the *Runcorn Weekly News*, very kindly included in his column my request for information about Runcorn Bridge and photographs of ICI locomotives. Ken Knowles of Weston, and Allen Mercer and Eric Carmichael of Runcorn, all responded with some useful information.

My hand-drawn maps and diagrams were made presentable by my son Simon, to whom I am also indebted for much advice and help with regard to photograph layout and chapter heading design in my own pre-publication book.

I owe much to my sister-in-law Anita Garnett, who is located relatively nearer to Birdswood than I am, and who has done much of the 'leg work' for me in my research. Her enthusiasm and unstinting help has been of great encouragement to me, in the course of which she had developed her investigational skills to a considerable extent.

A great deal of practical help was given by Grace Bunn, a lively 87-year-old with an alert mind and crystal-clear memory. Grace formerly lived at the lovely cottage over the tunnel end near to Birdswood and kindly made contact on my behalf with Edna Culshaw and Betty Huntbach. Edna made available a photograph of her late father George, while Betty let me have one of her late husband Joe, taken while he was working inside the second Weaver Junction box.

A host of photographers kindly responded with permission to reproduce some of their work. The include Dick Blenkinsop, David Cross, Hugh Davies, Ted Gray, Keith Miles, Brian Morrison, Derek Penney, Norman Preedy, Allan Sommerfield, Tim Shuttleworth, and Online Transport Archive. Yes despite my efforts to contact others whose work is used in these pages, I have not met with success; if they would kindly contact me via the publisher, their work can be duly acknowledged.

My gratitude must be expressed to Will Adams and the team at Silver Link Publishing, who not only agreed to publish this material but also kindly and patiently gave me much help and direction.

Finally, I am indebted to my friend Ron Williams of Devizes who, after carefully reading through my Birdswood project file with great interest, started the ball rolling simply by saying to me when he handed back the folder, 'You ought to write a book about this.'

Peter Haddock
Westhouses
Derbyshire

1
A HARD DAY'S NIGHT

There were just a few periods during the night shift when there was sufficient time between trains to allow you to become drowsy. With nothing else to do – except perhaps polish the handles of the signal levers, but who in their right mind would want to do that at 4 o'clock in the morning – it was really hard to keep awake. Sitting quietly on a locker away from the stove, the drowsiness was accentuated by the constant hiss of the Tilley lamp. The stove itself didn't help, kept alight summer and winter as the only means of boiling water to make the all-important tea. It gave out quite a lot of heat, to which the stove

pipe made a significant contribution as it rose vertically above the back of the stove before disappearing through the pitched roof some 6 feet or so above.

Outside the signal box was the stillness and deathly quiet of Birdswood. Not even the screech of an owl to ripple the undisturbed surface of this calm hour. Eyelids became heavier and the field of vision narrowed until it became impossible to keep the eyes open.

'Nothing wrong with just resting them for a few minutes,' I thought to myself, but what a mistake. Totally unaware that I had drifted off into sleep, my reverie was shattered when,

Birdswood box is seen from the up track of the Liverpool branch, the down track of which is out of shot on the right at a lower level. The low wall in the distance is the parapet of the flyover carrying the up Liverpool line over the West Coast Main Line, which lies to the left down the embankment. *R. Stephens*

unable at last to maintain a reasonable sitting position, my head slumped forward with a jerk and woke me up.

'How long have I been asleep?' I wondered. 'Have I missed any trains?'

No, that could not be possible with the ever-vigilant Mr Culshaw still calmly reading his *Daily Express*. It wouldn't do for me to fall asleep now, otherwise it would prove right his prediction that I wouldn't make it through the night shift. Determined to experience fully this hitherto unknown world of all-night railway signalling, I felt that now I had left school it was not only time to sample a 10 to 6 shift, but prove into the bargain that at last I had grown up.

While these thoughts were going through my mind I must have drowsed off again. Suddenly I was startled into action by the 'ding-ding-ding, ding-ding' of one of the instruments on the block shelf. But which one? And was it a 3-2 bell code? Yes, it was, I convinced myself. Springing into action, I noticed Mr Culshaw looking in my direction over the top of his reading glasses.

'Come on, Pete, jump to it – you'll have it entering section before you've answered the bell if you don't hurry up.'

He must have known I was shattered, having been awake since 6 o'clock the previous morning and having worked a full day at the ICI factory where I was hoping soon to begin an engineering apprenticeship. How I had managed to persuade my parents to allow me to do a night shift with Mr Culshaw I don't know, but agree they did. Now, at the unearthly hour of 4.00am, his good-natured chivvying was meant to encourage me to keep going, despite my tiredness. About 2 hours ago he had suggested I put my head down for an hour or two but, not wanting to miss any of the action, especially since this was my first night shift, I had declined and insisted on carrying on.

The nearest block instrument to me was the Down Main, but the tone was not right for that bell, so I guessed it was the Up Main and did my usual trick of flicking the bell with my finger to check the tone. Yes, that was right, so I returned the 3-2 code with a practiced forefinger on the key, then turned the knob

anti-clockwise, which moved the needle from LINE CLOSED to LINE CLEAR. This action unlocked the lever mechanism at Norton Crossing box, about 2 miles down the line towards Warrington, so that the signalman there could pull off his up signals to clear. The next thing was to offer the train forward to the signalman at Weaver Junction by tapping out the same 3-2 bell code on the Up Main instrument. Having done so, I stood back awaiting his acceptance. There was no reason for him not to accept this train, as nothing had passed in either direction for some few minutes and there were no trains of higher priority expected along the up Liverpool line. Sure enough, after about 15 seconds the Up Main line bell rang out its 'dong-dong-dong, dong-dong' and immediately the needle flicked over to LINE CLEAR. This procedure is not as long-winded as it sounds, the whole sequence being completed in something less than a minute. Now I could pull off my Up Main line signals to allow this unfitted freight train to pass through the section on its way to Camden.

Levers 13, 14 and 15 control the Up Main. They are not, however, pulled off in numerical order. Where there is a Home signal, a Starting signal and a Distant signal, the Home is always pulled first, then the Starter, and finally the Distant. That sounds easy, and levers 13 and 14 are, but the Distant is 1,470 yards from the signal box and is the most difficult lever to pull. For me, a fit 15-year-old, it was just about all I could do to pull off this lever without letting it slip back (which would have caused it to lock, thereby preventing it being pulled off), but I had developed a kinetic approach to the problem using my whole body weight to bring this lever over. As it was being pulled I watched the repeater instrument on the front face of the block shelf swing to 'off', confirming that this Distant signal, almost a mile away and out of vision, was now showing a green light in readiness for the train to pass. The road was now set for the passage of the freight train, but there is still much more to do in order to care properly for this train as it traverses the Birdswood section.

Next, details of the train must be entered in the Train Register, which is a record of all

This shot shows Fletcher-type block instruments in Weaver Junction signal box (identical to the four at Birdswood), which show the state of both the up and down lines in one casing . The bell is housed at the base between the four bronze pillars, and the signalman has his finger over the tapper, used to send bell codes to the next box. These instruments were manufactured by the London & North Western Railway in its works at Crewe. *Norman Jones*

trains passing through the section, and entries are made as events occur. Right now I only need to write up the code 3-2 with the time it was received and passed on. Since this is an 'unfitted freight' – that is, a goods train made up entirely of wagons that do not have vacuum-operated brakes, or has such brakes in use on less than four vehicles – it will run between 30 and 40 miles an hour. This relatively slow speed is due to the fact that the only braking force to stop the train is the combination of engine and tender brakes, those on the guard's van and the less than four vehicles with the vacuum brake in use.

It will probably be another 6 or 7 minutes before we can expect to see it pass us on the Up Main line, so I decide to sit down for a while and have a quick glance at yesterday's newspaper. However, while I have been busy with all that has been going on, Mr Culshaw has put the kettle on the stove and washed our mugs ready for another cup of tea.

'Do you fancy another cuppa, Pete?' he asked, when I had finished booking the train. 'It'll help keep your heavy eyelids in the right place!'

So he had noticed me nodding off on my unofficial duty! Even though it was only about an hour and a half since the last cup, my throat was drying out and I was more than ready for another.

'Yes, please, Mr Culshaw,' I replied, as he prepared the vintage brown earthenware teapot. Intending to have a quick look at the *Daily Express* while he was making the tea, I had just sat in his seat when the Norton Crossing signalman sent 2 bells, the code for 'Train Entering Section'. Right away I sprang to the block shelf to turn the knob a quarter turn clockwise, causing the instrument needle to flick from LINE CLEAR to TRAIN ON LINE, thus indicating to Norton Crossing box that the signal had been received. The time of this signal was then entered against the train in the Register. In just another 3 or 4 minutes the train would pass us.

Before it did, the tea was poured and a sandwich, left over from my 2.00am 'dinner', was produced from my lunch bag, but no more than a bite was savoured before the exciting sound of the freight train emerging from the short Dutton Tunnel was clearly heard on the still night air. It was time to attend to duty. The inner man must wait. I went over to the Up Main corner of the box and slid the window sash back to look towards the oncoming train, now approaching the Up Home signal. The headlamp at the base of the chimney with one over the left buffer could be clearly seen, which confirmed to me that the train was running under the right bell code. The fresh, clear night air of early summer was invigorating, and I remember thinking, 'I should have opened this window 15 minutes ago, then perhaps I wouldn't have nodded off.'

After a few deep breaths it was time to signal 'Train Entering Section' – 2 bells – to Weaver Junction, then back to the window to keep an eye on the train as it passed – most importantly, to ensure that, as the guard's van passed, the red tail lamp was clearly visible. But was it? Yes, it was.

'Tail lamp complete,' I called, turning my head back inside the box to Mr Culshaw as the guard's van passed beneath the flyover. Then, walking over to the levers but keeping an eye on that tail lamp, I waited until it passed the Up Starting signal. The train was now completely out of the Birdswood section, so the levers could be released, allowing the signals to drop to the 'on' (Danger) position. No great effort was needed this time. The next step was to ring 2-1 – 'Train Out Of Section' – to Norton Crossing and turn the needle to LINE CLOSED. But even now the job was not finished, as the Train Register had to be brought up to date by logging the times of the last two bell codes. In about another 3 minutes, perhaps a little longer, Weaver Junction would ring up 2-1 to us, indicating that the freight train had passed beyond that section, and the time of this vital last message brought our log in the Train Register to a completion for that particular train.

You may wonder just what is the significance of the remark 'Tail lamp complete'. Mr Culshaw taught me right from the beginning not only to look for the tail lamp, but always to let him know I'd seen it. When I first started visiting the signal box, he would look for it himself, but as time went on and he realised I was taking seriously my great privilege of unofficially working in a signal box, he developed a trust in my reliability and powers of observation. His clear direction to me was that I should call out 'Tail lamp complete' when the rear of the train passed, provided of course the lamp was visible. This came as a result of his excellent method of teaching me the operating procedures. He didn't simply tell me what to do, rather he coached me to reason out the proper course of action.

'What would it mean, Pete, if you didn't see the tail lamp?'

'That it had gone out!' was my first rather cocky reply, as though it was a silly question.

'But what if it hadn't gone out? What could that mean?' he probed.

'Oh, I see. Are you thinking that part of the train may have broken away?'

'Now you're getting warm. We don't know how many coaches or goods wagons make up a train, do we? So how can we tell if the train is complete?'

'Only if we see the tail lamp,' I replied confidently.

'Good,' he said, giving me that quizzical stare and half smile that often indicated there was another tricky question on the way. Such questions were intended to help me develop my ability to reason on what I already knew.

'So you didn't see the tail lamp and you assume part of the train has broken away. What would you do?'

Over the months that I had been visiting Birdswood signal box, Mr Culshaw had been teaching me the rules, and when I look back over my life I wonder if he was hoping I would join British Railways London Midland Region as a trainee signalman. If so, how disappointed he must have been when I started my working life at ICI Rocksavage Works with the prospect of becoming an indentured engineering apprentice. However, if he was disappointed, he never showed it, and all the time I continued showing interest in how to operate the box, he willingly carried on training me. At the time of his question, 'What would you do?', I had some knowledge of the rules and bell codes, so my mind went immediately to the fact that if the train that had just passed was in fact only part of the train, it must be stopped. This thought formed the basis of my reply.

'I'd send "Stop and Examine", seven bells, to the next box, then get on the phone to tell the signalman it had passed without a tail lamp.'

'Good try, Pete, but it's not right. There's a bell code especially for such circumstances. What is it?'

'A special code for no tail lamp? I can't remember that. What is it?'

Above Looking in the up direction on Saturday 24 April 1954, the line on the left is the refuge siding (which extends almost as far as Birdswood signal box), then follow the up and down tracks of the West Coast Main Line. The signal box stands on the embankment carrying the up Liverpool line over the two main-line tracks before joining the up main line at Weaver Junction; the flyover can be seen to the left of the bracket signal. The down Liverpool track lies at the other side of the embankment. The typical LMS bracket signal carries Birdswood's Up Home signal, with the distant for Weaver Junction Intermediate Block (or Outer Distant as we called it) beneath. The Down Main Starting signal with Preston Brook's Distant stands opposite. The tall Down Main Home signal can be seen in the left distance above the flyover. If you look carefully behind the telegraph post and wires to the left of the signal box, you will be able to see the Down Liverpool Home signal on its tall post, which has a repeater arm out of sight at lower level. *C. M. & J. M. Bentley*

Below Seen from the flank of the up Liverpool flyover on the evening of Saturday 23 July 1955, a boat train special to Euston from Heysham is hauled by filthy 'Royal Scot' Class No 46130 *The West Yorkshire Regiment*, the tender of which is just about level with Birdswood signal box. A view very similar to this could be seen when looking out of the signal box window in order to check that a passing train had the all-important tail lamp. *J. A. Peden*

Above On Saturday 15 October 1955 the 1.15pm Edge Hill-Willesden Class D freight hauled by Stanier Class 5 No 45451, due past Birdswood at 2.12pm, crosses the flyover as it heads south along the up Liverpool branch to join the West Coast Main Line just over a mile ahead at Weaver Junction. Birdswood signal box roof can be seen above the train just left of the apex of the platelayers cabin. Note the down Liverpool Home signal on the left of the curve, with its tall repeater giving an earlier sighting of the aspect. This view, looking northwards, gives a good indication of the layout and relative elevations of the Birdswood tracks. *R. J. Blenkinsop*

Left On Saturday 24 April 1954 an up through freight train, running under the bell code 1-4, leaves Birdswood territory heading for Weaver Junction with Bowen-Cooke 'G2' 0-8-0 No 49431 firmly in charge. These ageing yet gracefully simple locomotives had a distinctive exhaust sound that could not be mistaken for anything else. The down Liverpool line is in the foreground, with the up equivalent beyond the train on the embankment. *C. M. & J. M. Bentley*

Left A Liverpool Lime Street to Crewe stopping train hauled by Stanier 5MT No 45372 nears the end of the 2-mile falling gradient of the up Liverpool track. Nearest the camera is the down Liverpool track, then the down and up main, all of which are at a lower level than the track carrying this train. Weaver Junction lies about a mile out of shot to the right. *R. Stephens*

Above Looking in the opposite direction towards Weaver Junction, rebuilt 'Patriot' No 45534 E. *Tootal Broadhurst* effortlessly hauls the six-coach Crewe to Liverpool Lime Street express towards the Birdswood Down Home signal on Saturday 24 April 1954. *C. M & J. M. Bentley*

Below With plenty of steam to spare despite a leaking piston gland, Stanier 8F 2-8-0 No 48134 based at Willesden shed draws a lengthy fitted freight towards Birdswood along the down Liverpool line on the same day, likely heading for Edge Hill. The West Coast Main Line on the left is laid with flat-bottom rail, in contrast to the bull-head track carrying the train. The up Liverpool line runs along the top of the embankment on the left. At the rear of the train the Weaver Junction Intermediate Block signals – on the up lines only and known as Dutton Up IB Section – can be clearly seen, with a train expected along the up main line. The two colour-light Distant signals for the Birdswood section can be glimpsed to their right on the cantilever bracket above the down tracks. *C. M. & J. M. Bentley*

No 46239 *City of Chester* hauls its light load of eight bogies along the West Coast Main Line past the Birdswood Down Home signal and towards the flyover on Saturday 23 July 1955 en route to Scotland. Although it has no headboard, this train is likely the forerunner of what later became known as 'The Caledonian', a limited-load express intended to reduce delays due to modernisation of the West Coast Main Line. *J. A. Peden*

'I'm not telling you that! You'll have to look it up yourself in the Rule Book. Get it out of the desk.'

At this point I ought to try to describe the desk for you, just in case you run away with the idea that it was a piece of typical office furniture. Far from it, because remember we are back in the early 1950s, long before manufacturers began making the huge variety of furniture available today. No, the signal box desk was made in the railway company's own workshops, likely at Crewe, and consisted of a simple wooden box about 3 feet square and 12 inches deep at the wall, sloping down slightly towards the front. Rather like a school desk, this inclined lid was hinged, opening up to reveal a large storage area inside. It was designed to be used standing up, and consequently had sturdy timber legs at the corners, made from 2-by-2 planed material, nicely cross-braced along both sides and the back to give it rigidity. It was painted in typical LMS maroon, but much of this colouring had been worn off the writing surface by Train Registers being slid over it during the course of many years. At the wall side was a flat section where pens could be placed when not in use, together with the bottle of black railway-issue ink, although at the time we are concerned with, the 'Biro' pen was a new innovation and was just being brought into common use. The storage box under the lid contained an assortment of work-related items, such as the Rule Book, spare Train Register, a few boxes of detonators, a railway whistle, several copies of the Weekly Notices and various special notices that from time to time were issued to all railway servants. On this occasion I wanted the Rule Book, which I knew was always at the front right of the desk for easy retrieval whenever it was needed.

Opening the Rule Book to the part where all the bell codes are listed and fully explained,

I found that sure enough a special code had been set up for just such occasions. 'Here it is,' I said triumphantly. 'Train passed without tail lamp – nine bells.'

'Now you're talking,' said Mr Culshaw. His face broke out into a broad smile. If anyone had been looking in on our conversation, they may have thought I had asked the question and he'd given the right answer. But that was the nature of Mr Culshaw. A dedicated, life-long railway servant, he was delighted to be able to pass on almost a full working lifetime of his personal railway signalling experience. The rest of that conversation centred on the actions to be taken to ensure the safety of other traffic until the rest of that train was found. For example, the part that had broken away from the passing train could have become derailed and could be fouling the opposite running line, requiring us to stop the next train going in the opposite direction to warn the driver to 'proceed with caution' and to report his findings, if any, to the signalman at the next box. It may have been, of course, that the lamp had simply gone out or had fallen off the last vehicle of the train, or perhaps had not been put there in the first place. But in railway operations, nothing can be left to chance or be taken for granted. There is a rule or regulation covering every single eventuality. This may just give you some idea, then, of how important it is for a signalman to see the tail lamp of any train, night or day.

'Hands-on' learning sessions such as this occurred whenever anything happened that I had not dealt with before. I would be tutored through the situation so that full attention was given to whatever was happening, and this would later be followed up during the very next lull in proceedings by a question-and-answer session relevant to what had happened. Mr Culshaw would pose his 'what if...' questions, leaving me to reason on the principles I had already learned and to answer according to the knowledge I had gained, so that, hopefully, I would arrive at the correct conclusion. As you may well imagine with a novice signalman like me, when talking over the theory of the job I often got it wrong, but my tutor applied the wisdom of his 40-odd years of railway working to steer me away from the host of incorrect methods of doing things to how it should be done according to the Rule Book. For this I was very grateful, because not only could I enjoy the rare privilege of actually being present in a real working signal box at a place where two important routes diverged, but I was being given the chance to learn the job in much the same way as I would had I been employed by British Railways.

My schoolfriend Alan Looker sometimes visited the signal box with me, but he was never able to persuade his parents to allow him to work a night shift. Despite this, he went one better than me and actually joined the railway on leaving school and trained to become a signalman in the Warrington area. Sadly we lost touch when I went overseas, and I have many times wondered what became of him. Who knows, he might have ended up working in the Warrington power box before he retired. I wonder if he ever thinks back to those happy days we had at Birdswood.

Back on nights, it is now 4.10am and the passage of the unfitted freight train has blown away my drowsiness. The cup of tea and remainder of the sandwich have been enjoyed, and very soon now we could expect what would seem like a continuous procession of various freight, parcels and overnight passenger trains. This period of 10 or so minutes when we had only one train going through the section was to be the last of only a few such periods during the 10-to-6 shift, so I could expect from now on to be busy, with plenty happening all the time until the shift ended at 6 o'clock. However, I would have to be out of the box almost 10 minutes before then, so as not to be seen by Ernie Antrobus as he arrived to take over from Mr Culshaw.

But just a minute! How did I come to be in this situation, someone who was not employed by the railway yet learning how to operate this signal box on the West Coast Main Line at a point where the Liverpool line diverges away to the west? To answer that question I suppose we must go back in time to the early years just after the end of the Second World War, when the newly nationalised British Railways was in its infancy and things were very different. If we do that, we can start at the beginning.

2
HOW IT ALL BEGAN

I used to enjoy those walks on a Sunday evening. Starting from Holly Bank Road in Halton, there were just four of us usually, my schoolfriend Barrie Dunbebin, his father Albert and mother Evelyn, and me. With Mr and Mrs Dunbebin taking the lead and setting the pace, Barrie and I would bring up the rear, keeping a respectable distance between us and his parents to prevent them overhearing any of our schoolboy plots.

Occasionally we would stop to examine something that caught our eye, like the blisters in the road tar that always seemed to be begging us to burst them. Usually we obliged, gathering all the evidence on the ends of our fingers or around the ankles of our Sunday best socks. Sometimes there were things in nature that attracted our attention, such as a dead hedgehog or a flattened frog, but more often than not it was something that had fallen from a passing truck or a part that had become detached from beneath a car that fascinated and delayed us. The adults were used to our stilted progress, rarely having to call or look behind to see where we were. They knew from experience that we would eventually catch them up.

Two out of every three walks would invariably result in us walking, in one direction or another, the length of Station Road, a country lane connecting the A533 at Hallwood Farm to the A56 near Halton station, which was actually in the parish of Sutton Weaver. That Halton station was about 2 miles from the village of the same

name did not concern us in the slightest – we were not travelling by train – but what it did mean for us was that we would pass two good locations for trainspotting. Not that Halton station was much of thrill on a Sunday, being on the Warrington to Chester line and carrying very little traffic. Why, even on weekdays there was plenty of time to become involved in other things with no danger of missing the trains. What it did offer, however, was the most fascinating spectacle of the rear of the train disappearing into Sutton Tunnel, which lay about 400 yards east of our vantage point on the road overbridge from where we could look down onto the station platforms.

Even more mesmerising was the effect created when a westbound train was coming through the tunnel towards us, pushing in front of it a cloud of steam and smoke left by a previous train. It seemed that the tunnel portal would gradually disappear behind a small cloud of smoke, then suddenly the speeding locomotive would burst through this smoke-bubble and dissipate the 'fog' as it drew its train into the evening sunlight. This was made all the more interesting for us because the true identity of the engine could not be clearly seen until it was well outside the tunnel. Looking from the road overbridge in the westerly direction, we could see Frodsham Junction and the viaduct over the River Weaver and Weaver Navigation. At the junction the Chester to Liverpool line would curve away to the north, and although that aspect provided some additional railway

Right Lines around Halton

Bottom right Looking east towards the castellated portal of Sutton Tunnel, 1 mile 154 yards long, there us not a train in sight. The eastern ends of the platforms at Halton station are viewed from the road overbridge, and how well cared-for this section of the railway appears. My wife's uncle, Walter Claydon, was ganger of this length of track until his retirement in the mid-1950s, before this shot was taken on Saturday 25 May 1957. The track is the Manchester to North Wales line operated jointly by the London Midland and Western Regions of British Railways. The signal controlling the up line on the right is a former LNWR lower-quadrant type of timber construction, carrying the Halton station Home and the Frodsham Junction Distant arms. On the shorter 'dolly' is the arm controlling the entrance to a loop in which a freight train could be held to allow a passenger train to precede it to Frodsham Junction, half a mile behind the photographer. The Halton Starter signal is most unusual, as the Signal & Telegraph engineers have utilised an old lattice bracket post with an extension bolted on to throw the arm as near to the down track as possible, and low enough to be visible beneath the bridge. Notice the water column with its heater positioned on the end of the platform, and the well-worn path from the platform to the platelayers hut halfway to the tunnel mouth. Apart from the tall signal post needing a lick of paint, the whole scene indicates that someone cares for this section of line. About a quarter of a mile beyond the woods on top of the tunnel runs the London-Liverpool line, with Sutton Weaver signal box somewhere off to the right, and Yellow Bridge – one of my trainspotting venues – about a quarter of a mile off to the left. If we found things to be sometimes quiet at Yellow Bridge we would walk a further half a mile or so to this location to see what was happening on this line. *F. W. Shuttleworth*

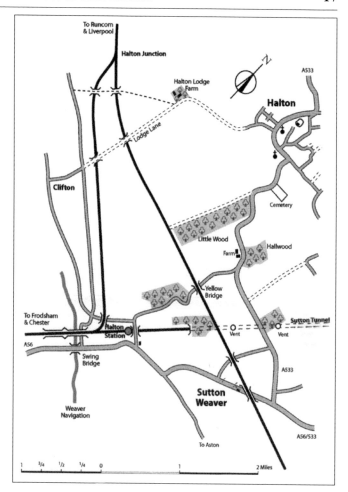

interest, the line was too far distant for us to be able to note any engine details. It must be said, though, that we were not missing all that much, because the locos tended to be mainly Fowler or Stanier 2-6-4 tanks, ex-Midland 4-4-0s, or 'Black Fives', with the very rare appearance of some rather more interesting motive power if a special train happened to be routed that way.

The other spotting location presented by this country lane was known locally as Yellow Bridge, a flat twin girder overbridge carrying the Liverpool to Crewe main line across our country lane. This was a much more interesting location from our viewpoint, because the line at this point was running along the top of an embankment completely clear of trees, shrubs and other things that conspire to hide trains from young spotters' eyes. Just to the west of this bridge stood a fine upper-quadrant splitting signal, carrying the Sutton Weaver Starting signal above the Halton Junction Distant on the main 'dolly', and the arm controlling entrance to a long loop on a shorter 'dolly' to the left. The loop line ran from here all the way to Halton Junction signal box, and was used quite a lot during weekdays to allow express trains an unhindered run down through Runcorn station, over the Mersey bridge and onto the flat south Lancashire coastal plain into Liverpool.

Nearly half a mile to the east of the bridge stood Sutton Weaver signal box, beyond which the up line descended a sharply falling gradient to Birdswood and eventually Crewe and Euston. At the base of the embankment at Yellow Bridge was a typical wooden railway

fence, which formed a natural perch for us whenever we paid visits here.

On the evening of our first walk past this spot, I remember Barrie and me being excited because we saw the Down Main signals were 'off'. Some hurried negotiations with Barrie's parents resulted in permission for us to stay and wait for the train.

'But not for too long, and be sure to catch us up before we get to Hallwood,' said his mother.

What would it be, passenger or goods? Could it be a 'namer' maybe, or even a 'semi', I wondered as we took up our positions on the fence. By this time it was after 8 o'clock and at that time in my life I had little idea of the traffic on that line on a Sunday evening. We waited and waited. When patience wore a bit thin, we scrambled up the embankment to look towards Sutton Weaver to see if anything was happening. Nothing. After about 5 minutes (which I'm sure you will appreciate is a long time for two impatient 11-year-olds) we decided that if we waited any longer we would never catch up with Barrie's parents before Hallwood, and anyway, even if the train came as we were catching them up, we could still see it fairly well. It never came, and we only just kept our word as we panted breathlessly up behind Mr and Mrs Dunbebin just as they joined the main road at Hallwood.

It was to be made quite clear to me some four years later when I began my association with Mr Culshaw at Birdswood that there was a very good reason why the Yellow Bridge signals were always clear on a Sunday evening when we walked past. Sutton Weaver signal box was 'switched out' at the end of the 2-to-10

On Saturday 20 June 1959 'Royal Scot' No 46147 *The Northamptonshire Regiment* hauls a down Liverpool express over Yellow Bridge, near Halton, my very first trainspotting venue. Station Road was the narrow country lane behind the hedge in the left middle-distance. Sutton Tunnel runs perpendicular to this line just beyond the trees by the end of the train. *R. Stephens*

shift on Saturday evenings until the start of the 6-to-2 shift on Monday mornings. In all fairness I'm sure eventually we would have tumbled to that ourselves had we spent more than just a fleeting visit to Yellow Bridge on Sunday evenings.

The walk sometimes took us down Norton Lane to Norton village. Well, hamlet may perhaps more accurately describe it, though it did have its own railway station, known appropriately as Norton station; sadly, after much of the north Cheshire countryside was swallowed up by the developing new town of Runcorn, it eventually became known as Runcorn East. To me it will always be Norton station, sitting as it does at the eastern end of

the Sutton Tunnel described earlier, on the same little-used Chester to Warrington line that, in pre-BR days, was operated jointly by the LMS and the GWR. Looking back in time, this fact seems rather strange to me, because while there was an abundance of ageing ex-LMS engines, I can never remember seeing any ex-GWR motive power on this line. It could be my memory playing tricks, but I feel sure that I saw an occasional ex-LNER 'D11' meandering along those metals.

The bridge at Norton station was a fine vantage point, which afforded an excellent view eastwards towards the village of Moore and Acton Grange Junction, as well as being aligned in the opposite direction with the east

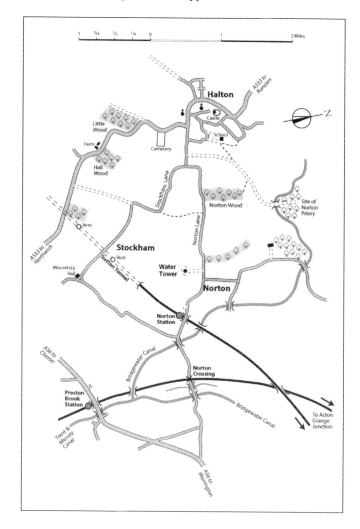

Lines around Norton

Norton station, in around 1956, is charming but somewhat neglected in this view looking towards Chester from the platform, virtually beneath the road overbridge. The little LMS&GWR Joint Type 1 signal box stands at the end of the up platform, while just out of sight around the corner lies the eastern portal of Sutton Tunnel, beyond which is Halton station, Frodsham Junction and Chester. *C. H. A. Townley*

portal of Sutton Tunnel. Added to all this, our elevated observation point gave a good overall view of both station platforms. If we wanted to walk onto the platform, there was a large open area to one side of the track divided from the platform by a beautiful paling fence, painted cream. The gate in this fence was always open, and as the station had no resident station master, there was usually no one present who would discourage our healthy interest in the line. A small signal cabin was situated at the tunnel end of the westbound platform, and I recall that there was a crossover just beyond the end of the platforms. Despite its long views, however, this was not a favourite spotting location, as we preferred to take the extra time to walk another half mile to Norton Crossing, where we were certain to see some 'real' trains on the West Coast Main Line.

A hundred yards or so beyond the station at Norton the road crossed the Bridgewater Canal by means of a hump-back bridge, and we would turn right just before it to walk along a very narrow lane towards Stockham and Sutton Weaver. Then turning right again into Stockham Lane, we were left with a 2-mile walk before reaching home. Unfortunately for Barrie and me as trainspotters, this particular route turned us nearly half a mile short of the West Coast Main Line at Norton Crossing, where there was, naturally for that time, a small signal box controlling the level crossing. We were, however, able to see in the distance trains travelling the main line between Norton Crossing and Acton Grange Junction, or rather the point where the Chester-Warrington line crossed over the West Coast

Main Line. Number-taking would have to be shelved until another time, as there was no way that Mr and Mrs Dunbebin would walk to Norton Crossing, only to retrace their steps if they did not wish a lengthy diversion that would have kept us all away from home until about midnight.

It seemed to me as a boy that Norton Crossing was miles from anywhere, but was splendid in its isolation. The only dwelling anywhere near was a small cottage right beside the crossing gates, which had been, at some time in the distant past, the crossing-keeper's home. On the Norton side of the main line were acres of fields surrounding two farmsteads, and the canal with its little hump-back bridge carrying the lane over the water, on the bank of which was a rather small whitewashed cottage. The railway through Norton station divided all this from the village of Norton itself, which appeared to hang on the hillside, with a huge sandstone water tower standing sentinel over this little community.

On the other side of the main line at Norton Crossing the terrain rose fairly steeply towards Daresbury village about a mile and a half distant, but only some 50 yards away from the crossing the Bridgewater Canal carved its level route around the hillside. At times the close proximity of this canal, which was carried over Red Brow Lane cut deep through the sandstone of the hillside, provided some distraction if interest in trainspotting waned, though it must be said that even from the canal bank 50 yards away, numbers could still be clearly noted.

It was at this location one fine day in 1954 that I managed to take a reasonable shot of an up express passenger train hauled by No 46148 *The Manchester Regiment*. As far as I can remember, this was my one and only foray into photographing trains, at least until much later in my life. Sitting on the railway fence beside the closed crossing gate (closed, that is, to road traffic, which was quite rare at this spot) the bells in the signal box could be clearly heard. Like all schoolboy railway enthusiasts, we soon got to know what the bell codes meant, which added to our interest, and we could even see the signalman working inside the box. On the rare occasions that a car or other road vehicle approached the crossing gate, the signalman would eventually come out with a huge Annett's key, open the gate farthest away from the vehicle, then walk across the line to the gate by the car. He would close this gate again immediately the car had cleared it, then would retrace his steps to close the first gate. This seemed rather odd to me, but in time, as I came to appreciate the dangers of a vehicle becoming stuck or stalling on a level crossing, the reason for this quite protracted procedure became clearer.

Visits to Norton Crossing in our early trainspotting days had to be on a Saturday or during the school holidays, when the walk from our village of Halton could be taken at a pace that suited us. That usually meant stopping here and there to look at something, or diverting into Norton Wood to see if the dam we had previously built across the stream was still there. Reflecting back to those times, it was rare for us to go directly anywhere, for whatever reason.

There is one particular visit to Norton Crossing that stands out from all the others. It was during the school summer holiday in 1949 when the weather had been consistently good (it always was in those days, it seems) that the terrible trio of Alan Looker, Barrie Dunbebin and myself arranged to spend a whole day collecting train numbers there. The travel details were simple enough. We would set off around half past nine and walk there. The important thing was not to forget to take some 'butties' with us, and since such things as Thermos flasks appeared only in the picnic baskets of the wealthy, we decided to call at my Uncle Jack's fish and chip shop to buy a bottle of pop each. Barrie and I both chose dandelion and burdock, but Alan fancied the recently introduced brew of American cream soda. I think each bottle cost fourpence, which included a penny returnable deposit on the bottle. These large bottles of mineral waters – to give them their proper title – were ideal for our purpose because they had a screwed stopper in the neck and could easily be resealed between drinks.

All business having been done, we set off along Main Street bound for Norton Crossing, each carrying in our gasmask bags our pop bottle and sandwiches, cake, apples and whatever else we had been given. Some may remember that these bags – surplus to requirements after the war – were commonly used by workmen to take their lunch to work. They were all a light khaki colour with an adjustable shoulder strap. We found them ideal for such occasions as this, because they had room for the ABC *of British Railways Locomotives* as well as our food and drink. The weather was ideal and we looked forward to 'copping' some 'namers', which we would not normally have seen on a Saturday. The walk was quite unremarkable, but inevitably we got into a discussion about who would dare walk round the parapet at the top of Norton Tower. It always happened, no matter who was with us.

'Bet you wouldn't dare walk round the top,' someone would challenge.

'Course I would!' came the reply. Then someone would chip in with some factual reassurance.

'They say it's wide enough to drive a horse and cart round it.'

'Who says that, then?' another would demand.

'My dad told me that, so it must be right,' said the informant.

Such a comment might interrupt the argument for a few seconds, until one of the protagonists would come up with the question that would inevitably put an end to the whole matter, regardless of how many times it had been discussed previously.

'Anyway, how would they get a horse and cart up there to prove it's wide enough?'

I have known that question to end up with the questioner finding himself tangled up with the hedge or, if we were going towards home, lying in the bottom of a dry ditch. On this particular occasion we were just about at the top of the hill leading down to Norton station, so the prospect of seeing something interesting on the Chester line took priority over rendering justice to the one who proffered the last question. And don't forget, too much larking about could end up with somebody's pop bottle being broken.

As we neared the bottom of the hill and rounded the bend the slightly elevated Chester line came into view, and just then a slow freight train hauled by an ex-LNWR 'Super D' 0-8-0 was approaching the bridge near the station. Though I have come to admire these fine old workhorses, at that time we spotters wouldn't give them the time of day, so seeing one then caused no flickers of excitement for any of us. That particular one was rather scruffy into the bargain, but I'm sure that had it been something else – even just a 'Black Five' – one of us would have sprinted the 150 yards to the bridge to take its number. The remaining half-mile or so to Norton Crossing was taken at a quicker pace as we were now within sight of the West Coast Main Line and could see some traffic on it. The sooner we got there, the less likely we would be to miss something good. Over the canal bridge now, with the railway getting ever closer, this last few hundred yards of country lane was flanked by fields of ripening grain. At last we arrived at the crossing gates.

We always preferred sitting on the far side of the track, which meant passing through the kissing gate beside the brick-built coal and ash bunker, then pausing to make sure the lines were clear before walking across. This pause was always used as an excuse to stare up into the signal box, especially if – as was usually the case during warm weather – the door was open. Not that we saw anything worthy of special mention when we did stare, but there seemed to me to be something of an 'aura' about a man who, by pulling a few levers and ringing some bells, could exercise authority over the magnificent speeding giants we had come to see.

Once across the line, we chose our perch on the wooden fence flanking the road. This side of the track was so much better as an observation post because there was nothing to obstruct our view of approaching trains, whereas on the Norton village side the view was foreshortened by a hedge to the cottage on the down side and the coal bunker and signal box on the up side. The only way our view from this side could be improved was by sitting on the crossing gate itself, but sometimes the signalman would not take kindly to that practice. No, we were far better off on the Daresbury side of the track. Whenever our perch on the fence became too hard to bear, there was always the flank wall of the bridge over the stream some 15 yards away. The wall was quite low, and the sandstone parapet wide, which afforded an almost armchair-like alternative to the creosoted railway fence. It was easy to see both the up and down signals and hear the bell codes from there; also, because we were just a little further away from the tracks, cab-side engine numbers could be more easily read.

Having set ourselves up for the day at this spot, we settled down to some really serious spotting. I suppose other groups of lads elsewhere did the same as we often did to make sure we took down all the relevant information. One would note the smokebox number and count how many coaches there were. Another would look for the shedplate and check the nameplate if the engine had one. The third would take the cab-side number. After a while, these duties would be rotated.

On this particular day there was nothing very remarkable about the rail traffic, but after settling into this business-like routine we decided it was time to have a swig of pop, just to keep us going until we had our lunch. Sitting on the fence, we could just reach down to take the bottles from our bags, hanging by their straps from the fence posts. The smooth taste of dandelion and burdock in a dry throat on a warm summer morning has to be experienced to be appreciated, so much so that it was indeed more than just a swig I was taking. At that moment, the only thing that could better the experience would be a Royal Train triple-headed by a streamlined 'Coronation' Class engine, a 'Princess Royal' 'Pacific' and one of the new diesel-electric locomotives, Nos 10000 or 10001. What an outrageous dream! But that obviously was not to be.

While these dreamy thoughts were passing through my mind, the peace and quiet of Norton Crossing was suddenly shattered by a loud and sickly cry.

'Uuuugh!'

This was followed by the sound of running water and a sudden leap from his perch on the fence by Alan, who made for the other side of the narrow road, spitting into the grass verge, still holding his opened cream soda bottle in his hand. He just stood there, stock still with head bent forward, looking down onto the grassy verge, occasionally retching and all the time ignoring our puzzled enquiries about what was the matter. By this time we had come down off the fence and had joined him on the other side of the road.

After what seemed like several minutes, but was probably only 20 or 30 seconds, Alan turned round to face us, wiping his mouth with the back of his hand and looking rather sorry for himself.

'What's the matter?' asked Barrie when Alan eventually stopped spluttering. 'Don't you like the new pop?'

I thought Alan was going to explode as he thrust out his hand holding the pop bottle. 'Pop? Here, you have a sniff at this and see if you think it's pop,' he said, handing his bottle to Barrie. Both Barrie and I smelled at the open bottle labelled 'American Cream Soda' and came to the conclusion that it was anything but! In fact, it smelled just like petrol. No wonder he leaped down off the

fence when he tasted it! Now we understood his uncharacteristic behaviour of spitting and retching. Since none of us had yet started to smoke, we had no matches with us, otherwise there would certainly have been a little experiment carried out using the foul-tasting contents of this bottle. We soon came to the agreement that the bottle did indeed contain petrol, not cream soda as stated on the label.

We shared our pop with Alan – more of a mouthwash than a thirst-quencher – and felt that this incident had cast a shadow over our day out. We therefore decided to return home to Halton and confront Uncle Jack about the petrol. This was obviously going to call for some diplomacy, because in order to earn some extra pocket money I sometimes used to work for him in the chip shop, putting potatoes into the peeling machine and afterwards using the hand-chipper. Clearly any careless accusations could cost me my part-time job, so the matter had to be carefully thought through and presented. When it was put to Uncle Jack, he was extremely apologetic. It seems that he had put some petrol into empty pop bottles for later use in his motor-bike, and somehow these bottles of petrol had become mixed up with supplies of mineral waters of assorted flavours that the manufacturer had fairly recently delivered to the shop.

Reflecting on the day, we felt that despite the incident with Alan and the 'cream soda', we had seen one or two good engines during that morning, so it had – we thought – been worth the long walk. On top of all that, Uncle Jack gave each of us a large bottle of pop free of charge. This time Alan chose ordinary lemonade, just to be on the safe side.

On Sunday 21 December 1958 un-named 'Patriot' No 45542 hauls an up express over the level crossing heading for Birdswood. The incident with the so-called cream soda took place just to the right of the white-painted crossing gate. The Chester-Warrington line, running across the horizon between the signal box and the train, was too far away from here for engine numbers to be noted. *B. Woodward*

3
FURTHER AFIELD:
LIVERPOOL LIME STREET

During those heady days there were times when we felt the need to pack more into a day of trainspotting than would occur naturally when we sat on a fence or a grassy bank alongside the track waiting for things to happen. True, there were some occasions when quite a lot would happen, but that would depend largely upon where we chose to go. If we went, for example, to Norton Crossing and sat it out alongside the West Coast Main Line, we could expect to see at least eight trains an hour, but if Halton station was our chosen venue for that day, less than half that number would be seen. For the most part it did not seem to matter how many trains we saw, the important thing was being in the vicinity of railway activity of some kind.

I remember on one occasion at Halton station we were totally absorbed in watching a porter repainting the white edge to the station platform. You could be forgiven for thinking that such an operation would not even fall into the category of 'activity', especially the pace with which it was carried out at such a remote country station in the days before 'time and motion' studies were heard of, yet we found it fascinating as we monitored the porter's progress from the road overbridge. This observation point gave a fine view of both platforms with the exception of the short stretch that lay directly beneath the bridge. As I recall, we were totally unobserved by the porter for some time, and it was only when he reached the end of the platform and turned

around to return to the station building that he noticed us on the bridge.

How could such a simple matter capture our attention between trains? Well, quite frankly it was the brush. The porter had what looked like a galvanized mop bucket in which he carried the lime wash, and from this bucket projected a handle giving the casual observer the impression that it was a mop. However, there had to be some secret device for making such beautifully straight lines along the platform edge, not only painting about 8 or 9 inches of the horizontal surface of the platform, but also treating the vertical face of the edging stones, which were about 3 or 4 inches thick. On some previous occasion the man had repainted the edges on the station building side to a point just beyond the overbridge, and as he recommenced his task – unaware of three pairs of eyes watching his every move – the secret of his obvious success was revealed. The bucket was carefully placed on a good-sized piece of cardboard at the platform edge just ahead of where he was repainting, so as not to drip any lime wash onto the surface of the platform, and when he drew the handle out of the bucket, all was revealed.

It looked for all the world like a sweeping brush with soft bristles, which of course it was, but the clever thing about it was that half the head of another soft broom had been nailed to it at right angles, forming an L-shaped brush that painted the horizontal surface and the vertical surface at the same time. The short piece nailed on the end also acted as a guide to give a perfectly straight edge to the whitening on the platform surface. The porter was careful not to overload his brush with too much lime wash, otherwise he would have splashed it everywhere, but he handled the device with great skill, and clearly – even though he seemed quite slow – was a conscientious worker. His steady progress along the platform edge with his secret weapon held our undivided attention for quite a few more minutes until he reached the lower end of the ramp, the job completed.

It was quite obvious, then, that if we wanted to enjoy a higher level of activity, we would need to do something about it. We would have to go further afield. I remembered once having been taken by my parents to New Brighton for a day at the seaside, our journey taking us by bus from our village of Halton to Runcorn station, then by train to Liverpool Lime Street. A short tram ride soon had us at the Pier Head, where we took the Mersey ferry to New Brighton. For me it was a fascinating journey, but the part that stuck in my mind was the awesome experience of Lime Street station.

This very busy terminus rang with the sounds of a lively railway, amplified by the sounding-board of the cathedral-like roof. The smell of smoke, steam and hot oil, together with that distinctive aroma of the moquette upholstery and wood veneer of LMS coaching stock lingers in my nostrils even to this day. Porters shouting, carriage doors slamming, engines hissing steam from their safety-valves as they waited impatiently for the 'right away', buffers clanging as the little station pilot marshalled coaches into and out of the platforms, the whine of electric platform tractors and the phut-phut-phut of the Lister-engined variety hauling a string of trailers laden with mailbags and all sizes of boxes and cartons, the piercing whistle of an engine about to haul its train out of the platform and into the dark, smoky tunnels beyond, the metallic clang of the upper-quadrant starting signal arm bouncing back to the 'on' position after a train had departed – all these sounds and smells mean so much to any railway-lover.

For me, this kind of venue was the place to be if a great deal of activity was expected. Add

This photograph, taken on Saturday 18 July 1964, shows well how Platform 7 extends way beyond the ends of the other platforms, only a few yards from where the tunnel starts. Here an unidentified 'Peak' 1Co-Co1 diesel-electric stands at the head of express 1N67. Steam is represented on the right by the station pilot, with the two arched roof spans forming the trainshed in the background. *Photographer unknown*

Top A scene familiar to all schoolboy trainspotters, and witnessed at every main-line terminus in Britain. On Saturday 25 September 1954 'Jubilee' Class No 45603 *Solomon Islands* could – by virtue of its name – mentally transport a spotter to the sunny climes of the mid-Pacific, a far cry from its home shed at Edge Hill. The group of eight schoolboys sits on or stands around the platform barrow, with an older man observing from beside the pillar. A corridor-end closure stands against the stonework behind the boys, while the whiff of steam above them belies an engine standing in the adjacent platform out of shot to the left. In the platforms to the right, two Stanier 'Black Fives' stand at the head of local trains, while a third train awaits its engine. In the bottom right-hand corner can be seen the end of a treadle, which, when a train is fouling the points, prevents the points lever from being moved and operates a warning indicator in the signal box. *J. A. Peden*

Middle Standing at the head of an eight-coach express train, 'Jubilee' No 45630 *Swaziland* is about to depart for Crewe and Birmingham on Saturday 16 July 1960. The lack of platform activity would indicate that all passengers are aboard, and the cylinder drain cocks are open, ready for departure. An early Reliant three-wheeler, the pride and joy of one of the station staff, is parked against one of the supporting columns near to where some recent repairs have been carried out to the platform edge and support wall. *J. A. Peden*

Bottom What a contrast from steam days! This shot, taken on 7 July 2004, shows Platform 7 as seen from the buffers end. Note how clean the roof appears, and the sturdy central pillars supporting it. The Virgin 'Pendolino', No 390047 *Virgin Atlantic*, has just arrived from Euston, whereas the Central Trains Class 170 'Turbostar' standing at Platform 5 on the left is the all-stations train from Crewe. *Author*

to those sounds and smells the wonderful sight of a clean, shiny maroon 'semi' of the 'Princess Coronation' Class, a 'Princess Royal' or even a 'Black Five', all beautifully turned out with crisp lining and gleaming paint, and you had a cocktail that any rail enthusiast would savour. Even the station pilot was a credit to the engine cleaners at Edge Hill shed. The constant comings and goings of 'namers' hauling express trains from and to various parts of the country was sometimes quite difficult to keep up with. Without a doubt, we had come to the right place if the number of engines seen was the important thing!

Both Barrie and Alan had been on the train to Liverpool before, so they may well have had the same sort of memories of that cavernous station as myself. For that reason, it was not difficult to persuade them that we ought to work hard on convincing our parents that we were mature and responsible enough by now to undertake such a journey without adult supervision. We reasoned that this task would be made easier if we were prepared to save up our pocket money and pay our own fare. In my case, that would mean saving for several weeks, as the return fare was 1s 10d, and I only received sixpence a week. Alan was an only child, while Barrie was the youngest of two brothers, so with their respective parents being reasonably well off, they would have been financially ready for the outing long before me. Besides, I seem to remember at that time still being in debt for smashing someone's window with a cricket ball, so the plans for our adventure to Lime Street station had of necessity to be long-term.

Thinking back to those days, we three trainspotters must have been rather like wizened old men in our approach to obtaining parental approval, because we developed a strategy for gradually getting parents used to the idea before we actually posed the big question to them. For instance, we thought it would be a good idea to start by asking our Dads how long the train journey to Lime Street would take, then a few days later asking Mums if they had ever noticed any schoolchildren travelling on the train without parents. We knew they would have to say 'yes' to that, because there were boys attending private schools around Chester or Liverpool who could be seen on the local trains on any weekday. Thereafter, it would only be a matter of days before we would declare our hand, reasoning that if we presented a really well-prepared case, having thought out all the different angles about the trip, they could hardly refuse their consent. In my particular case, it was imperative to somehow get a rise in pocket money as soon as possible, otherwise the trip would have to be on a Saturday after we had started school following the summer break, and we desperately wanted to go on a weekday.

My plan was to offer to chop sticks for lighting the fire for our household and for my granny, who lived next door, over and above my normal chores of filling the coal bucket early each evening. Mother never said as much to me, but I believe she was impressed with my offer of chopping sticks for granny (her mother), because she put my case for increased pocket money to Dad in such a way that he could hardly refuse. The campaign was won! From the following Friday – which was pay-day for my Dad – my pocket money went up to ninepence a week, which doesn't sound much but was in reality a 50 per cent increase, making possible a midweek trip to Lime Street station before the end of the school holidays.

Our plans centred around spending as much time as we could on the platforms at Lime Street, because no doubt we would stand a good chance of 'copping' some engines that might otherwise take us many months of ordinary spotting to see. We would therefore need to take a lunch with us, as refreshment room food would have been beyond our resources. It was decided, though, to buy a drink on the station at Lime Street. The next thing to be agreed was which train to catch. There was the option of a local train, either the Chester-Liverpool or the Crewe-Liverpool, both of which would probably stop at all stations en route. Alternatively, there was the more exciting option of catching the 5.00am Euston-Liverpool express, which would depart from Runcorn at 9.53am and stop only at Allerton and Edge Hill before reaching Lime Street at 10.24am.

We opted for this train in the hope that it

Our train journey to Liverpool started from this platform about eight years before this photograph was taken. On Saturday 20 June 1959 an up Lime Street to Birmingham stopping train powered by Stanier Class 5 No 45002 enters Runcorn station, having just crossed the River Mersey and Manchester Ship Canal by means of William Baker's magnificent high-level bridge, seen just to the right of the engine. From the end of the platform the line is built on a viaduct leading to the Mersey bridge, and the extent of the slope away from the station is indicated by the roofs of the houses just beyond the Starting signal. *R. Stephens*

would have a good engine hauling it, a choice which in the event turned out well because it was double-headed. The train engine was 'Patriot' Class No 45512 *Bunsen*, which we had seen numerous times before, but the exciting pilot engine was a bright and shiny 'Princess Royal', No 46207 *Princess Arthur of Connaught*, clearly fresh from a visit to Crewe Works. Probably the reason why it had been coupled to this train as pilot was in order to return it to Edge Hill shed. For me this lovely locomotive was a 'cop', but Barrie and Alan had seen it before. It was nevertheless exciting for all of us to be travelling on a double-headed express bound for Liverpool.

Now, as a logical-thinking schoolboy, as I believed myself to be, I could never come to terms with the name of that 'Princess Royal' engine. I had never come across a girl named Arthur in all my 14 years, and though I knew some girls with rather unusual names, Arthur was not one of them. So why, among a class of 13 excellent and graceful locomotives, all except one carrying nameplates, should *Princess Arthur of Connaught* be the only male name in a list of females? These powerful, magnificent locomotives could often be seen on the Liverpool-Euston expresses, frequently hauling 17 or 18 coaches well filled almost to overflowing, and were the longest locomotives on the London Midland section of British Railways, apart from the 2-6-6-2 Garratts that were used mainly on the Toton to Brent coal trains. The only unnamed engine in this class was No 46202, the turbine-driven locomotive designed by Sir William Stanier and known as the 'Turbomotive'. But why the anomalous *Princess Arthur of Connaught* was so named remained something of a mystery. Even if someone had been able to give a reasonable explanation, it would still have seemed ridiculous to me that the engine was so named and that a princess should have a name like Arthur!

The reasoning behind opting for the express to Lime Street was that it would give us more time on the station. By contrast, we planned to return by a slow Liverpool-Chester train that stopped at all stations, thus prolonging our railway experience for that day. The intervening time on Lime Street station, however, was a trainspotter's wonderland of activity that, if it had been some form of drug, would have had all three of us as high as a kite! The amount of activity was so overwhelming that at times it was difficult to note all the numbers, even though we had seen the engines. We worked out a method for dealing with all the movements that were taking place. One of us would spend some time at the end of Platform 7, which stretched furthest from the buffers into the station throat, and from where most of the movements into the station could be seen. Numbers of all locomotives would be noted and later compared to the list of numbers taken by the other two of us as we wandered around the station platforms and concourse. One advantage of being on this lonely 'duty' was being first to spot engines from Edge Hill shed reversing down through the dark tunnels into the station to be coupled onto their express trains. The other two, located down near the buffers, would probably be aware of these light-engine movements but would be too far away to note any numbers.

After about half an hour we would change duties so that no one would become lonely or feel he was missing out on something. I personally never enjoyed this lone vigil, feeling that if I missed something very important I should never be forgiven by my pals. It was so much more interesting wandering slowly around the platforms together, comparing notes on our personal observations, enjoying the warmth, smells and sounds of the various locomotives as they arrived and came to a stand just short of the buffers.

Being able to stand so close to those fiery monsters was a great thrill, touching them and sometimes standing by the cab, looking longingly up into the face of the smiling driver or fireman, hoping beyond all hope that he might invite us to step up into that hallowed area, the driving cab. Never once did that happen, much to my disappointment, and it was only as I grew older and – I believe – wiser that I realised the reason why. So many good railwaymen were proud of their work in such an important section of the transport industry, even though it had fairly recently been nationalised, and they were well aware that if the interest of schoolboys such as Barrie, Alan and myself could be captured, there would be a continuation of school-leavers intent on making a career for themselves on the railway. In such a place as a main-line terminus, however, there was always bound to be the watchful eye of someone in authority, such as the Station Master, Inspector, Running Foreman or other official, who would frown upon schoolboys being allowed onto the footplate of an engine, even though it was at the end of its journey and trapped in a position in front of the buffers until the train was hauled out, freeing it to run light-engine to Edge Hill shed for attention before another duty.

Had we been more careful in our planning of this expedition, we would have opted for the earlier Chester-Liverpool train, which departed from Runcorn at 9.07am and, after only one stop at Ditton, reached Lime Street station at 9.33am. We would then have been on hand to witness the formation of the crack 'Merseyside Express' to Euston, usually hauled by a 'Princess Royal' Class engine but very occasionally by a locomotive of the 'Princess Coronation' Class, known to us as 'semis'. This name was derived from the fact that these engines, originally built with streamlining, had a slightly flattened, oval curvature at the top of the smokebox to accommodate the bull-nosed casing. When the streamlined casing was removed, this flattened smokebox top was revealed, creating the impression that the locomotive was semi-streamlined. I can remember seeing only one streamlined engine – painted blue – which, according to my memory, was No 6227 *Duchess of Devonshire*. The record books, however, claim that only the first five streamliners were blue, the rest being maroon. My only explanation for this is that because I saw this engine from a distance, I mistook the final digit of the cab-side number for a seven, when it could have been a four. I was alone at the time, returning from a short visit to Yellow Bridge, and saw the train as I neared Hallwood Farm. Perhaps my distance vision was not as good as it should have been, but that engine was certainly blue. All these years I have always thought of that engine as *Duchess of Devonshire*, but if it had been No 6224 it was named *Princess Alexandra*.

There were of course other expresses departing from Lime Street for such diverse places as Birmingham, Newcastle, Glasgow, Edinburgh, Perth, Aberdeen and Inverness, as well as to Euston, all having named engines, mostly of the 'Royal Scot', 'Jubilee' or 'Patriot' classes, which, together with the 'Princess Royal' and 'Princess Coronation' classes, formed a fairly good variety of express passenger motive power.

It may be difficult for some to realise just how exciting it was for three 14-year-olds to be able to spend virtually all day in such a location as this noisy, busy, bustling main-line terminus, because for most people a visit to such a station is merely an inconvenient part of the overall journey. But for us it was almost heaven, like a huge magnet that was steadily attracting the warm oily metal of main-line steam engines and their smaller cousins, the shunters and station pilot. It must also be remembered that there is more to railways than engines, coaches, signals and lines. This included such everyday things as the immense station clock mounted high on the glazed arched end of the overall roof, and the W. H. Smith bookstall with its wide variety of books, newspapers, magazines, sweets (now that rationing no longer applied) and – on the better railway bookstalls – railway books including the famous ABC, which was to become the locospotters' 'bible'. There was

On a beautifully sunny morning some time in August 1959 an up express bound for the West of England pulls effortlessly away from the platform at Runcorn behind 'Jubilee' No 45669 *Fisher,* which is in a remarkably well-turned-out condition. Even the Mark I coaches carry a sparkle. There is much evidence of work in progress prior to electrification, which would considerably hamper the running times of trains on the West Coast Main Line and the Liverpool branch. *Derek Penney*

also the 'mechanical horse' vehicle, with its single central front wheel and able to 'turn on a sixpence', used to haul detachable trailers to ferry mail, goods and other items from the terminus to the premises of customers in the nearby area, and the fascinating destination board, which showed the departure times of trains, their destinations and the platform from which each would leave, being wound on periodically by the Station Foreman, who inserted a brass handle in the side to roll up the blind on which all this train information was printed (was that not a measure of stability?). The situation is rather different now, because one almost expects to hear the dreaded announcement, 'This is a platform alteration'. Then there was the Refreshment Room and the various Waiting Rooms, which were rather like a station within a station, with people coming and going in a constant procession. We also noted the little group of porters and other railwaymen who gathered from time to time on one of the platforms to take a break from their mailbag sorting, packing-case shifting and trolley loading, enjoying a cigarette and a cup of tea before the next rush occurred.

All these facets of railway life were so absorbing to the three of us that we could have spent the whole day and more wandering about this railway 'Mecca', but, not wishing to be late home for tea, we decided to make the journey back on the 4.25pm Shrewsbury train, which stopped at Edge Hill only, due at Runcorn at 4.49pm, instead of the all-stations slow train as planned. That would give us the choice of walking from the station over Top Locks to the Egerton Arms to catch the 5.05pm North Western bus for Northwich, getting us to Halton by 5.15pm, or walking to the Cleveland Hotel in Greenway Road to get the Crosville bus for Warrington, which would drop us at Halton at 5.25pm. We opted for the North Western service, not because it was earlier, but because there were a good many more Crosville services in the area, whereas the North Western service, centred on Northwich, was only 2-hourly. So most of the

buses we were likely to ride in were the green Crosville Leylands. Besides, there was the added attraction of riding the red and cream North Western Bristol K5G double-decker.

So we came to the end of a perfect day. Well, almost, because it was marred by one small incident that – at the time it happened – seemed quite serious to a hungry schoolboy. Mother had packed me a nice lunch of corned beef sandwiches and three big chunks of her special 'parkin', a cross between treacle cake and ginger cake. One chunk had earlier been promised to Barrie in return for one of his Eccles cakes, and one to Alan as a swap for a piece of his mother's iced sponge. I had eaten the first three of my four corned beef 'butties' and was relishing the thought of the last when the accident happened. We were sitting side by side on a four-wheeled station barrow enjoying our lunch, and just as I reached into the brown paper bag and took out my last sandwich, Alan shouted, 'Look at that!' He was pointing over towards Platform 1, where a shining 'Jubilee' was drawing in with the morning Glasgow express. Amid all this excitement my last sandwich dropped to the dirty platform, fell apart and was judged after scrutiny to be unfit for human consumption. Alan was quick to offer me one of his sandwiches containing home-cured ham to make up for my loss. What a gallant gesture that was, appreciated even more in retrospect than it was at the time, but it gives some indication of the camaraderie that existed as we enjoyed that special day out together.

Eventually home after our tiring but exciting day, having enjoyed my tea (as the evening meal was called), all that remained to be done was to underline in my *ABC* the engines that had been seen for the first time that day. Having done that, I made my way upstairs to bed. I felt as if I had been working hard all day at a task I thoroughly enjoyed, and was looking forward to a night's rest. It was not too long before I fell into a very deep and contented sleep.

There are no prizes for guessing what I dreamed about that night!

4

THE RAILWAY 'METROPOLIS': CREWE

In the days when steam ruled as king, probably every trainspotter in the land would have wanted to make at least one visit to what was perhaps the best-known railway town in the world – Crewe. Not that there is anything particularly special about the town itself, because prior to the railway works being set up there by the Grand Junction Railway in 1840 it was merely another small village on the Cheshire plain. No, it was simply the fact that Crewe had been fully developed as a railway interchange station forming the hub of an intricate network of lines to various parts of the North West of England. Naturally, the more lines there were, the greater the likelihood of there being plenty of traffic. Add into the equation two engine sheds – or motive power depots, to be more precise – together with a complex railway works, and the attraction became so strong for those devotees of locomotives and trains that they were drawn from all quarters of the country.

In order to paint a picture for those readers who have never been to Crewe – can there really be such an enthusiast? – I shall briefly describe some of the features of this rail 'metropolis'. The West Coast Main Line slices south to north right through the centre of Crewe, 158 miles from Euston. Joining from the south-west is the line from Shrewsbury and mid-Wales, while tracks from Stoke-on-Trent and Derby converge from the south-east. Both these routes meet the main line south of the station at Basford Hall, which was the location of a huge sidings complex as well

as Crewe South shed. Immediately north of the station and just to the west of the running lines was Crewe North shed, very conveniently located for the many express passenger locomotives that needed to be coupled to their trains in the station platforms. Clearly visible from the platforms are the tracks leading off north-east to Manchester and north-west to Chester and North Wales. In addition to all this is the loco works located to the north of the Chester line, which generated a good deal of traffic and brought here some engines that would not normally operate in the area, for example 'Jubilee' Class locomotives used on the St Pancras-Leeds route.

Such was the mix of traffic, routes and engines that to go trainspotting at Crewe was simply a must for any railway enthusiast. Despite modernisation, and electrification and simplification of the trackwork and platform layout there, the magnetic effect of this 'metropolis' is still drawing trainspotters and photographers more than 50 years after my first visit, as I have personally witnessed during my many travels through the station in the latter years of my working life.

As this 'magical' station was located merely 20 or so miles from my home village, it should not be surprising that the desire to visit and get in on all the action there grew stronger and stronger as my interest in railway matters increased. Yet unlike Liverpool, Manchester or my county town of Chester – where I had been with my parents on shopping or sight-seeing trips – the only reasons to visit Crewe would be either to watch the railway at work or to catch a train to somewhere else. At this particular time, in the late 1940s, I had not the slightest idea that on two occasions in the early 1950s I would be changing trains at Crewe in order to travel to Scotland, and although out of chronological order, perhaps I may be permitted to tell you about those two occasions first.

In 1952 my older brother, who was serving in the Fleet Air Arm, was posted to Lossiemouth in Morayshire, Scotland, near the lovely city of Elgin. He and his wife Dilys invited our family to visit his married quarters on the outskirts of Elgin to spend a holiday in that beautiful part of Scotland. My younger brother Robin and myself accompanied our parents on what was – then – the longest train journey I had ever made. Naturally I was very excited about the trip, especially as the journey north was to take place overnight, and involved a change of trains at Crewe. I had been to Crewe a year or so before this time, as the rest of this chapter will divulge, but this was at night, which made the journey all the more unusual. We were to travel on a Friday night during early August.

My friend Alan Looker's father ran a Ford V8 Pilot as a taxi, which conveyed the four of us and our luggage from home to the railway station at Runcorn in good time for us catch the 8.01pm stopping train to Crewe, where we arrived at 8.45pm. A rather long wait at Crewe gave me the chance to look at some of the engines on trains I would not normally see in the daytime, yet some of the regular engines seemed to turn up even at this hour. It was approaching dusk by now, which meant that any trains not using platform lines were rather more difficult to see, but that did not detract from my enjoyment of this new experience. Our scheduled train to Scotland was the 7.15pm sleeper from Euston, which arrived at Crewe at 10.14pm with 'Princess Coronation' Class locomotive No 46253 *City of St Albans* at its head. I noticed that it was almost immediately uncoupled from the train, so clearly we were to have a fresh engine for the journey over the border, but by the time I had to board (Mum was getting concerned by this

time that I might be left behind) it had still not reversed down onto our train, so I was unable to note the details. I did, however, feel it couple on just a few minutes later.

There was a great deal of station work done in those 15 minutes before the train resumed its journey northwards, most of which I witnessed from the platform and – nearer to departure time – the vestibule window. As well as the usual handling of mail bags out of and into the vans, the restaurant car was shunted off the train and the various water tanks were replenished. I had not seen any sleeping cars close up before, and I recall thinking at the time that it was such a waste of time sleeping during a train journey. Had I been a businessman and not a schoolboy I might have felt differently.

Our train departed from Crewe right on time at 10.29pm, and I recall getting quite excited about the fact that this would be the very first time I had travelled past Birdswood on the West Coast Main Line. It was, in fact, during that leg of the journey that I first realised that I was unable to sleep while travelling by train. Anyway, who would want to miss any of the things that took place on the railway even at night? Although the darkness obviously prevented my seeing much of the countryside, I was aware of a rather leisurely pace, and do not recall any station stops before Perth. However, there was a pause of several minutes at a place where there seemed to be several tracks but no platforms that I could see, and I came to believe subsequently that it may well have been Carstairs, where a portion of the train destined for Edinburgh could have been detached. I recall the fairly slow climb northwards from Perth to the highest point for any main railway line in the United Kingdom, Druimuachdair, 1,484 feet above sea level, then drifting downhill into Aviemore where we arrived just after dawn. Changing trains here, we took the local train to Elgin, passing through places with such romantic names as Boat of Garten, Grantown-on-Spey and Forres.

Our return journey took place in the daytime, which gave me the opportunity to actually see some of the places we had previously travelled through in the dark. Crewe once more worked its magic on me, but this time we had only a short wait for the Liverpool train as far as Runcorn. My then future wife Joan and I made a similar journey to Elgin in 1955, but unfortunately for us we were caught out by the railwaymen's strike on our return, the train from Inverness, which we caught at Aviemore, proceeding only as far as Glasgow. There were to be no trains south to England until the following day, so we were forced to spend the night in the hotel overlooking the station. It is a good thing that my brother George insisted on lending me some money in case such a delay arose, as the strike was due before we began our return journey but no one was able to tell us how the timetables would be affected.

Now let us step back in time to preparations for my first journey to Crewe, which was for the sole purpose of trainspotting in the company of Alan Looker and Barrie Dunbebin. Not prepared to wait until school holidays for this trip, it would have to be on a Saturday. We were not mercenary, but we obviously had to consider the cost of such a trip, which would have set us back 3 whole shillings for a return ticket. So the trip would have to start with saving a few weeks' pocket money in order to buy the ticket. Then there would have to be plans for food and drink, which my mother would have to arrange some time in advance because – remember – we are back in the days before most households had such a thing as a refrigerator. Any meat for our sandwiches would most probably be Spam from a tin, because the weekend joint would all be gone by Monday. Just as in the case of our earlier trip to Lime Street station at Liverpool, we decided to take just 'eats' and buy something to drink at Crewe.

Alan's Dad had agreed to find out the times of Saturday morning trains for us when he took one of his fares to the station at Runcorn. The choice was fairly limited if we were not to be too late getting there, so we opted for the 8.00am train from Liverpool to the West of England, a Saturdays-only train calling at Runcorn at 8.25am and arriving at Crewe at 9.03am. To give us enough time to walk from the bus stop by the Scala cinema in Runcorn to the station and buy the ticket, we would

Judging by the slam-door coach immediately behind the tender, this is a local express from Liverpool Lime Street to either Crewe or Chester, starting away from Runcorn station some time in 1960. The Stanier Class 5 engine, No 45449, appears to be in ex-works condition and could well be rostered on a short running-in turn after overhaul at Crewe. The end of the down platform at Runcorn can be seen beneath the bridge arch, with the branch off to Folly Lane sidings and the ICI complex veering off left past the AWS-type signal box. Some catenary support posts have been erected in the station area as part of the electrification programme, and the 20mph permanent way slack, together with the many concrete duct covers at the trackside on the right, indicate that much work is in progress at this time. The track has been cut through red sandstone, typical of this area, and the train is passing beneath the bridge carrying the footway between Picow Street and Balfour Road. *R. Stephens*

have to be on the Warrington to Weston Point bus leaving our village at 7.40am. Getting up in time was never a problem when there was something exciting to do, which was the case on that Saturday, so leaving home a good hour earlier than when we were going to school was built into our programme.

We had a quarter of an hour or so on the station before our train arrived, but the only engine we saw was the 350hp diesel-electric shunter working on the Folly Lane branch to the ICI factories at Weston Point, and a 'Super D' 0-8-0, which hauled a freight from the Lancashire side of the Mersey and, after running through the station, set back into the Folly Lane sidings. Our train arrived on time, in the charge of 'Jubilee' Class No 45622 *Nyasaland*, which had us at Crewe a couple of minutes before our scheduled time of 9.03am. We were thankful that our journey was only a short one, as the train was full and we had to stand in the vestibule all the way.

On getting out of the train it was like stepping into another world altogether. I believe one has to be a rail enthusiast to truly appreciate the special atmosphere that was Crewe station in the heyday of steam. Wherever you looked, all you could see was the railway. You could smell that rather special odour that can only be experienced when in very close proximity to something connected to the railway. Here in this huge wonderland of transport there was sufficient to more than satisfy even the most voracious appetite for all things railway. There was nothing grandiose, like the train shed at Paddington or York, nor anything of great architectural merit like the magnificent frontage to St Pancras station, but what could be seen here was a genuine, down-to-earth everyday railway with so much to see that one could spend 24 hours a day being absorbed by what was happening. In fact, I did once read of a group of trainspotters who – to the surprise of station staff and some train crew – spent all day and all night soaking up this rather special ambience.

On reflection after many passing years, and being perfectly blunt about Crewe at that time, it was rather a hotchpotch of station buildings that gave the impression that things had been added as the need arose, rather than being planned in advance. For example, between the track serving Platform 1 and the non-platform line next to it (I believe it is officially known as Down Through No 2 Road) there was a screen, the purpose of which was to protect passengers on Platform 1 from any rain from the west. The bottom of the screen was 4 feet or so above rail level, so if a locomotive passed by on that through line all that could be seen of it was the lower parts of the wheels, with the important bit of the cab side where the number was displayed being totally obscured. There were, however, some most fascinating details to be seen, such

Although Crewe station itself lacks the grandeur of other stations such as St Pancras, Paddington or York, there are some items of architectural merit, such as the bow windows of the Cafeteria and Waiting Room on Platform 5, which carry some nice details such as the double-round-head sashes within each opening, and the decorative sandstone and special brickwork. Yet the trainshed roof seems very ordinary – almost factory-like – by contrast, and even Lime Street station can boast a roof structure more worthy of the photographer's attention. *British Railways*

Above This photograph illustrates the usefulness of the footbridge at the north end of Crewe station, with access to all platforms. On 20 August 1955 Ivatt Class 2MT 2-6-2T No 41229 awaits departure with the 12.38pm local service to Northwich. *Brian Morrison*

Below Although taken on Friday 19 August 1955, when remodelling was under way, this photograph, taken from the footbridge, provides a clear view of all the tracks coming in from the north, demonstrating why it was such a favourite spot. No 46235 *City of Birmingham* draws into Platform 4 with a southbound express. Crewe North shed (5A) is the building on the extreme left. *Brian Morrison*

as the fine bow windows to the Cafeteria and Waiting Room on Platform 5, together with the matching stonework around all the other openings. But we must not lose sight of the fact that we are here to see the trains, not the buildings!

There were plenty of passengers standing around on the platforms when we alighted from our packed train, and, having stood in the vestibule, we were first off just as soon as the train came to a stand. Instinctively we gravitated towards the end of the platform, which was where we were likely to see the engines bringing trains to this busy station. Of course, not all of them had the engine on this end, because if they were travelling south the train would stop with the locomotive at the south end of the platform, but you don't have to be a brilliant mathematician to work out that about half of them are heading northwards, so the engine would be somewhere near the platform end. We did notice that a long footbridge spanning the ends of most of the platforms, which was outside the train shed at this end of the station, seemed to have attracted about a dozen or so schoolboys. Realising that it must be a good vantage point, we climbed the steps to sample the views from this elevated position. It did not take many minutes for us to appreciate the advantages of this lofty look-out post.

It was so much quicker and easier to move from one side of the station to the other by means of this bridge. If a locomotive in the distance appeared to be heading along one of the through lines on the eastern side of the station, it was no problem – if we wanted a better view – to simply walk along the lattice bridge to get nearer to it as it passed. In the meantime, nothing was obscured from view, as it would be by the flank walls or steel plating of the usual type of bridges, so there was never the anxiety of missing something while changing positions. Another great advantage of this footbridge was that it was rarely used by passengers changing platforms; they tended to use the other bridge nearer the middle of the platforms.

After a short while we felt thirsty, so decided to get a cup of tea from the Refreshment Room. Even though it was not yet time for 'elevenses', our hunger and thirst momentarily prevailed over the desire to spot as many engines as possible. Despite all the usual music-hall jokes about railway tea, that obtainable at Crewe was pretty good, though obviously not up to home standard, and was very much enjoyed by us all, together with a Kit-Kat that Mum had put in my lunch bag. We agreed that while down from our high observation platform we would explore the rest of the station to find out if there were any other reasonable spots from which we could see most of the trains. At the south end of the platforms it was fairly good, but being at platform level meant that every time a train came or went, our view across part of the station would be momentarily obstructed. So after about half an hour we decided that it would be better for us to go back to the footbridge at the north end, where one train movement about every minute would keep us well and truly occupied.

Some time during the late morning I overheard some lads nearby talking about a visit to the shed – Crewe North Motive Power Depot – which was situated not far away from the west end of the footbridge. Alan and Barrie agreed that we should find out more about this, so we enquired of the boy who had mentioned it in the first place. He in turn pointed out to us a young man in long trousers (which in those days meant he had probably left school) who was standing at the foot of the steps on Platform 4. When we got nearer to him I realised he had well and truly left school, appearing to me to be in his early 20s. He was surrounded by a small group of schoolboys who were giving him their rapt attention. We were just in time to hear him say, '…so be at the bottom of the steps on the west side of the footbridge for 1 o'clock when we shall be escorted into the shed by one of the officials.'

Just as he turned to move down the platform, Barrie asked him, 'Excuse me – can anyone go to the shed?' The man replied that he was looking after a group from a youth club in Shrewsbury and had a letter from the Shedmaster giving permission for a guided tour at 1 o'clock. He seemed to be pondering over whether or not to allow us to join his party, then said, 'How many of you are there?'

Barry told him there were only three of us, to which he replied, 'All right then, you can come with us. Five of our boys failed to turn up this morning, so you can take their places. But don't let us down. You must follow right behind us as we are taken through. No lagging behind or getting up onto any engines. The foreman who is guiding us said it will be no longer than 10 minutes. Is that clear?'

Barrie agreed that it was, so in about an hour's time we would be seeing inside the famous 5A shed. Maybe this would be the great chance to see some engines we had never seen before.

It didn't seem long before our stomachs were calling for food, so we agreed to go down onto the platform end to sit on one of the many four-wheeled barrows to eat our lunch. There was plenty for us to see from the north end of Platform 3 so, apart from anything on the eastern side of the layout that was hidden from our view by other trains, we didn't miss a lot. All this time the page in my little hard-backed notebook was gradually filling up with the numbers of locomotives I'd seen that day. Before we had time to make another visit to the cafeteria for a drink it was about 5 minutes to 1 and already some of the Shrewsbury party were assembling by the footbridge. Not wishing to miss this golden opportunity of the shed visit, we decided to leave the drink until we came back, so joined

On Saturday 16 June 1951 'Princess Coronation' Class 'Pacific' No 46224 *Princess Alexandra*, based at Polmadie, hauls the up 'Royal Scot' into Crewe and, although not booked to stop here, has been routed alongside Platform 5 rather than the centre line between Platforms 4 and 5 usually allocated to non-stop trains. One can almost feel the excitement of the short-trousered trainspotter as this giant engine glides through the station. Originally built with streamlined casing, the engine still carries the cut-down smokebox top. *C. M. & J. M. Bentley*

On the same day an up express from the North Wales coast runs in off the Chester line behind Stanier Class 5 No 44714 piloting an unidentified ex-Midland Railway three-cylinder Compound 4-4-0. Note the clerestory coach in fourth position, which may indicate that running staff had been hard pressed to find sufficient coaching stock for Saturday seaside specials such as this. However, the very clean condition of the pilot engine shows that someone had time available, or was it that the loco had just been released from the works after repairs, as the tender seems quite grimy? The flat concrete roof of the ARP-style Crewe North signal box is clearly visible above the train. *C. M. & J. M. Bentley*

this little group of unknown lads to await our guided tour.

Shortly afterwards, the young man Barrie had spoken to earlier arrived and carried out what can only be described as a roll-call. Was he a schoolteacher or something? He certainly had the ability to keep his group of boys in order. After he had called out the names of his party and heard their affirmative 'Yes, Sir!' he added, 'And the three stragglers? Oh, yes, I see you're here. Good.' He then went into his warning address that he had earlier given to Barrie, at which time a rather solemn man in a trilby hat and raincoat came up and said he was our guide. He also went through a short warning speech before we set off line astern behind him, Alan, Barrie and myself forming the end of the tail. At first there was a timber path that crossed several tracks and led in the direction of the shed, but just before we got to a door in the side of the shed we had to pick our way over a couple more tracks before entering.

My first and abiding impression of the inside of the shed was one of gloom. I am not sure what I expected, but perhaps adequate lighting would have been one thing. However, the reality was that if there was any light at all, it was daylight that filtered in through smoke-blackened windows in the roof and walls, which made the grubby engines standing dead in their stable seem like cold, dark giants. Here and there I noticed a solitary light bulb aglow, but the effects of continuous smoke inside the building made everything merge into one. Only the clean engine numbers painted boldly on the cab side sheets stood out from the pervading gloom. It's a good job they did, because after all that is why we were there, but writing those numbers in the notebook in such gloomy conditions was not easy, especially as we had to keep one eye open for any trip hazards and open pits while maintaining a fairly rapid pace following our trilby-hatted guide. Nevertheless, nearly a full page of numbers were noted on that quick tour.

It was only some time later that I came to realise that, yes, I had seen those engine numbers, but how much of the engine had I actually seen? Little more than the lower part of the huge driving wheels and motion and the actual number itself. As for the general shape, colour, chimney style and other details that could be picked up at the lineside during a normal spotting trip, all that was lost in the gloom of the shed. Though I did get the opportunity for another shed visit during a later trip to Crewe, I passed up the chance, preferring to stay on the footbridge or platforms. To this day I feel an aversion to the insides of motive power depots, and am unable to generate much enthusiasm for the myriads of published photographs showing locomotives at rest. I admit that there is some merit in such photographs for the purpose of study, but for my taste I would much prefer to see these mighty giants out on the track doing the job for which they were designed and built. So clearly I was not cut out to become an ardent 'shed-basher'.

Another visit to the cafeteria for a cup of tea slaked our thirst, then it was back to the footbridge and the more serious business of trainspotting. Sadly, during the time we were in the shed we missed the down 'Royal Scot' as it cruised through the station on its non-stop journey to Glasgow, almost certainly hauled by a 'Princess Coronation' 'Pacific'. However, there were many other delights to be savoured that day, one of which was witnessing the non-stop passage of the up 'Royal Scot' hauled by the 'black twins', the country's first main-line diesel-electric locomotives, Nos 10000 and 10001. What a fine spectacle that was, just a few minutes before we boarded our Crewe-Liverpool local train back to Runcorn. I had seen these diesels on many occasions since their introduction and was fascinated by the shape and sound of them. Little did I know then that some 20 years later such sounds would be quite normal on our railway system.

All in all it had been a very good outing, well worth saving for, and a journey I would make again several times before I left school. As for locos that I had not seen before, there were several 8Fs, 'Black Fives' and various smaller 0-6-0 engines, but nothing in the way of 'namers', as I expect most of them had been out on their various diagrams when we were visiting the shed. One further little detail that our trip put right for me: if anyone asked if I'd ever been to Crewe, at least I could now say 'Yes'.

5
FINDING THE FIRST TREASURE

There are two subjects never very far from the thoughts of most schoolboys – sport and trainspotting – and both feature prominently in their conversations with friends. Since sport has been dealt with by many other writers, I therefore focus attention on railway matters without any apologies or qualms of conscience .

Especially after weekend forays into the realms of trainspotting, there always seemed to be plenty to talk about at school on Monday. It was a wonderful feeling when telling envious school pals about the rare 'namer' seen during a spotting trip, especially if it was an engine not normally seen at that location. At some of my favourite haunts such sightings were not unusual, because engines being run in after overhaul at Crewe Works were sometimes rostered for a Crewe-Liverpool Lime Street stopping train, or possibly a Crewe-Preston turn, with similar fairly local low-speed trips for freight engines. Seeing a 'Jubilee' that would normally be rostered on the LMS Midland Division expresses from London St Pancras to Derby or Nottingham generated great excitement. Having seen such a 'cop', one wished it were Monday morning back at school – even though it was mid-Saturday afternoon on a lovely summer day – so that this startling piece of railway intelligence could be casually related to one's friends.

It was precisely because of one such conversation during the Monday dinner break at school that the whole course of my life was changed by a casual remark passed by a boy listening to our railway chatter. Graham Bunn was not a particularly close friend, because he lived so far away from my village of Halton, but at school he joined in all the usual games and activities. On that particular day Barrie Dunbebin, Alan Looker and I were chatting to a few other classmates about our trainspotting the previous weekend, when Graham – quite out of character for him – interrupted the discussion with an almost casual remark:

'You should see the railway lines where I live!'

The conversation halted immediately. A long silence ensued while those profound words sank in. We were all aware that Graham lived somewhere away from the village, because we never had his company outside school hours, but exactly where he lived was never really established. Could he possibly live somewhere so exciting that he had trains passing by his home? After what seemed like many minutes, but in reality was only about 10 seconds, Alan asked, 'Lines? How many lines are there?'

'Four,' replied Graham proudly, 'and they're all main lines, too.'

A shocked silence ensued as this startling comment struck deep at our hearts. I personally would have given my right arm to live alongside such an important railway line, and doubtless the others would have too. Only when the full import of Graham's claim had sunk right in did the conversation resume.

'Don't believe you,' Alan said.

'Get away!' remarked Barrie.

'Impossible!' That was how I felt.

These retorts came out almost simultaneously from three different mouths, above each of which a pair of eyes had widened with astonishment.

'Four main lines. Did I hear you right? There's nowhere round here with four main lines,' reasoned Barrie. His comment summed up our total disbelief in what Graham had said, though we had absolutely no reason whatsoever to think he was not telling the truth. But incredible as it sounded to us then, the truth of the matter just had to be established. By this time I had decided that I must pay a visit to this interesting location, so I would have to find out the details.

'Where's that, then?' I asked after a few more seconds of silence.

'Birdswood,' replied Graham with an assured air, 'and the main line from London to Scotland goes nearly past the door of our house.' His demeanour visibly changed as he said that. It was as if he had instantly grown a couple of inches, and cocking his head to one side as if to challenge any of us to dispute it, he went on in this same, uncharacteristic, rather challenging way. 'Why don't you come down on Saturday to see for yourselves?'

We looked at each other as if to gauge the reaction to that suggestion, probably having already decided to do exactly that, when Barrie eventually broke the silence by asking, 'How do we get there?'

'Easy,' said Graham. 'All you do is get the Northwich bus to the Talbot Arms at Dutton, then walk down the boat road to our house. There are only three houses near the end of the canal tunnel – ours is the whitewashed one on the left.'

That sounded too simple to be true, but before we could question Graham about the finer details, he said, 'Knock on our door, then I'll take you to where you can see the trains.'

'I thought you said the lines ran past your door,' protested Alan, who was beginning to wonder if all this was some cock-and-bull story, 'and now you say you'll take us to where we can see the trains. They either go past the door, or they don't,' he logically concluded.

'They do go past the door, but I mean I'll take you to a good spot where you can see them better,' said Graham. 'But to see the Liverpool trains we'll have to cross the Scotland lines.' Then as an afterthought, perhaps sensing our shock at the prospect of crossing over some busy tracks, he added: 'Don't worry, there's a public footpath, so you are allowed to cross the line there.'

The effect this revelation had on our school work for the rest of the week could probably be measured in terms of teachers' comments if they wrote weekly reports on students instead of just one at the end of term. Speaking for myself, I can say that I found my concentration on the House of Stuart, square roots and the various provinces of Australia was somewhat lacking. I was so preoccupied with the thought of seeing expresses rushing to and from Scotland as well as Liverpool, all at the same location, that lessons for the rest of that week were endured rather than enjoyed, and – on reflection – that very week may have been significant in the battle between Barrie, Ronnie Ellis and myself for the honoured place at the top of the class. The rivalry for first place in class had always been between Beryl Povey, Ronnie, Barrie and myself, but Beryl managed to pass the eleven-plus and therefore went to the Helsby Grammar School. That was a move I should have liked, as the Chester and North Wales line from Manchester via Norton ran behind the school, but for me it was not to be. Now with Beryl out of the running and Ronnie not interested in trainspotting, I found myself that week at a distinct disadvantage, speaking from an academic viewpoint.

Friday seemed an age in coming, but at last we finished school for the week and could concentrate without any distraction on the serious business of our proposed expedition to this delightfully named Birdswood. Barrie had developed a very keen interest in photography, so would no doubt take his camera, which could be useful, though supporting his expensive hobby on only schoolboy pocket money would probably mean he would take no more than one or two snaps. On the way home from school by the longest route we knew, to give us time to fully

The road in the foreground is the A533 from Northwich (to the left) to Runcorn, with the Talbot Arms at Dutton in the bottom right-hand corner. The 'boat road' starts almost opposite and runs diagonally between the hedges towards the top left-hand corner, beyond which Birdswood signal box lies well out of shot. Dutton Tunnel is just off to the right, running beneath the A533. Taken in the early 1960s, this shot shows the support masts for the overhead line equipment along the railway, with some new ballast scattered. It appears that the up refuge siding has been lifted. The train seems to be a mixture of open short-wheelbase wagons, a tanker and a couple of soda-ash containers. The buildings between the main road and the boat road are all part of Smithy Farm and Smithy Garage, belonging to the Hazlehurst family. *Author's collection*

discuss such an important matter, we carefully planned our strategy for this long-awaited trip to Dutton.

'How long does the bus take to get to Dutton?' asked Alan.

'Well, it's only about five minutes to Sutton Weaver, so to Dutton should only be about another five,' replied Barrie. Having driven along that road with my father many times I knew that the Talbot Arms was only a mile or so from Northwich Corner, as we called the parting of the A56 and A533. Older people we knew referred to this junction as Potts' Corner, because Arthur Potts and his father before him lived in a bungalow situated right at the junction.

Barrie went on, 'We'll have to get the bus home in time for tea, so if the ride takes ten minutes, and the North Western goes through Halton at ten to five, we'll have to be at the bus stop in Dutton just after half past four. How long does that give us at this Birdswood place?'

'Depends on how long it takes us to walk to Graham's house and back,' I replied. 'Didn't he say we had to walk down the boat road?'

'He did, but I've never heard of this boat road,' was Alan's reply.

'Even if it was a mile, it should only take us about a quarter of an hour, so between half

past one and half past four we do half an hour's walking, which leaves us about two and a half hours for trains,' said Barrie.

'That should be plenty of time to see what it's like,' I said, 'and if it's no good we can catch the earlier bus home.'

Then Alan came up with the big question. 'How much is it to Dutton?' The success or otherwise of our trip to this new spot surely didn't depend on money? And if it was only about a 10-minute ride it couldn't be all that much. Anyway, however much it would cost, the trip had to be made.

'Graham said it was fourpence return,' I recalled. That seemed to calm matters down, and we confirmed our agreement to catch the quarter past one bus next day.

Travel arrangements duly made, we felt our week at school had been worth it, even though we all had trouble paying full attention to lessons. Now we had that lovely Friday afternoon feeling, with a good weekend in prospect and a new trainspotting location to investigate. Just think, four main lines! That should be very busy, but what Graham really meant was four tracks of main line, quite another matter. Even so, we felt excited about our trip and hoped it would live up to our expectations.

The so-called 'boat road' turned out to be a

narrow gravel track, just about wide enough for a car to pass along. It had been provided as a means of walking barge-horses from one end of the tunnel on the Trent & Mersey Canal to the other, while the barges were 'legged' through the tunnel by the bargee and his family in the days before barges were fitted with engines. There was, of course, no towpath through the tunnel itself. Part of the way along this track was a circular dark-red brick ventilator, through which the motor of a barge passing along the canal beneath could sometimes be heard. On each side of this track the blackthorn hedges were kept in good condition by being occasionally 'laid' by the farmer. After about 300 yards the track dipped into a hollow and twisted around a small copse. Through the gaps between the trees we could make out a typical post-and-wire fence, often used as a boundary alongside a railway track, which caused us to quicken our pace because now we must be nearing our goal. Then suddenly the quietness of the countryside was shattered by the roar of an express train, which seemed to appear from nowhere, travelling at a very fast pace hauled by a beautiful maroon locomotive. We were too far away to get the number, but there was no doubt that it was a Stanier 'Pacific' of the 'Princess Coronation' class. The maroon coaches carried nameboards, illegible to us at that distance. While the express train sped south we three were racing through the copse toward the fence, where we arrived just in time to see the last coach flash by into the distance. What a thrilling introduction to this new venue, though we were still only on our way there, so to speak. Graham Bunn's house was a further hundred yards along the track. But already any doubts we may have had about the truthfulness of his claim were well and truly dispelled.

There were two red-brick cottages to the right of the boat road and a whitewashed cottage to the left, right beside the portal of the canal tunnel. This interesting cottage was where Graham lived with his family, and it was perched almost directly over the end of the tunnel. Graham was waiting for us when we got to the door, so right away he guided us towards the so-called Birdswood. We walked across a gravelled yard onto which the three dwellings fronted, then passed through a stock-proof gate in the railway fence and climbed the rising path away to our left, which brought us into a narrow, elongated meadow right alongside the railway lines. We climbed up onto the wooden fence and sat taking in the scene. Directly opposite where we were sitting was a stout signal post on the far side of the tracks, and it carried a red Starting signal with a yellow Distant arm beneath. There were all the usual chains, cables, pulleys and counter-weights around the base of the signal post, and the usual access ladder fixed to the rear side of the equipment. It seemed such a long way to the far side of the tracks, as we had never before been to any location where there were more than two tracks, one up and one down. It was after these details had been seen and mentally noted that I counted the number of tracks running past that point. Three! But didn't Graham promise that there would be four?

Such a serious shortcoming had to be pointed out to Graham, who quickly explained that we were sitting alongside the main line from Euston to Glasgow. Warrington, Preston, Carlisle and Scotland were away to our right, with Crewe and London to the left. He explained that the third track, nearest to us, was a siding that was not often used. As seasoned locospotters we should have realised that the rails were not as shiny as the up and down running lines. Immediately to our right was a lovely LMS-style cantilevered signal carrying the up home and a distant beneath. The cantilever threw the 'dolly' out over the siding to give drivers of up trains as early a view as possible of the signals.

So where were the lines to and from Liverpool, as promised? Our expert local guide soon allayed any fears we had, explaining that we needed to move about 150 yards to our left to reach the spot he'd been talking about. That location was hidden from our view by lineside shrubs and a few trees. We were just on the point of climbing down from the fence when the up Home signal cleared, so we decided to hang on until the train had passed. A few minutes later we heard the distinctive

Above 'Princess Coronation' Class 'Pacific' No 46246 *City of Manchester* is at the head of the up 'Caledonian' on 20 May 1959, and is passing milepost 175¼, about 200 yards short of the Birdswood Up Main Home signal. The track nearest the camera is the up refuge siding, not often put to use. Just in front of the milepost the gradient post indicates a change for this train from an uphill climb of 1 in 180 from Preston Brook to a level track past Birdswood. The field at the top of the cutting on the right belonged to the uncle of the girl who eventually became my wife. As trainspotters we would walk to the bus stop in the village by way of this field, so that we could stay near the railway for as long as possible. This habit was based on the dread that the best engine of the day was the one that passed just after you had left your spotting location. *N. Preedy archive*

Below 'Jubilee' Class 4-6-0 No 45583 *Assam* – not so immaculate as *Prince Rupert* mentioned in the text – coasts down the incline with a West of England express and almost totally obscures Birdswood signal box as it runs along the up Liverpool line towards Weaver Junction on Saturday 25 July 1959. Just above the rails to the right of the telegraph pole can be seen the Up Main Home signal with the Weaver Junction Outer Distant (IB) beneath in the on position, indicating that this train will have a clear run onto the West Coast Main Line at Weaver Junction. *J. A. Peden*

sound of a three-cylinder exhaust beat approaching from our right, getting louder and louder as it came around the slight bend into our vision. A 'Jubilee' Class engine, No 45671 *Prince Rupert*, in immaculate condition stormed past at well over 60 miles an hour, hauling the ten maroon coaches of the 11.58am Southport-Euston train. It had been climbing for slightly more than 3 miles after passing over the level section at Moore where the water troughs were situated. The steepest section of the climb between Norton Crossing and Preston Brook was almost half a mile at 1 in 112 which, for a locomotive of this class with a load of only ten bogies, presented nothing more than a slight challenge. The 'Jubilees' were very attractive and could easily be distinguished from the 'Black Fives', or 'Mickeys' as we called them, by the fact that their chimneys were slightly taller and therefore appeared slimmer. These lovely engines belonged to one of the largest classes of named locomotives on the whole of British Railways, 191 in all, each with a name able to conjure up in the mind of a young schoolboy an adventure to some faraway island, such as No 45569 *Tasmania* or perhaps No 45609 *Gilbert and Ellice Islands*. Other engines might bring the day-dreamer face to face with such historical figures as Nos 45639 *Raleigh*, 45645 *Collingwood* or (one of my favourites) 45670 *Howard of Effingham*. It may be argued that such giants of steam were helpful in fixing in my mind certain historical or geographical details that would otherwise have seemed much less important.

Climbing down from the fence, we agreed that we were going to like this fine location, and Graham led us along through the narrow meadow to a place where it widened out into a nice, flat clearing with a wood bordering the left side and far end. A fairly high wooden railway fence stood to the right alongside the tracks. At this point our view of the railway – by now just the up and down main tracks – was not obscured by any lineside shrubs. But the outstanding feature of that location was a fine maroon and cream signal box built on a brick base high on an embankment right in front of us, with a railway line running right alongside it. On a board mounted on the gable

end the name BIRDSWOOD could clearly be seen. Magnificent! Graham told us that although this was a good spot, we couldn't see any trains on the down Liverpool line, but pointed out the public footpath that we could use to cross the line if we wanted to. No, we decided it was reward enough just to stay here and take in our new surroundings. Anyway, absorbing all these wonderful experiences one at a time would perhaps help us better appreciate them, and we could always use that footpath on some later visit. Graham, having other things to occupy him that day, then left us to our new-found thrills and made his way home.

Our excitement was enhanced by being able to hear the bells ringing in the signal box, the windows of which were open on this

The up Liverpool line runs directly alongside the box, with the other tracks at lower levels, down Liverpool to the left and up and down main to the right. The sliding windows used to rattle when an up Liverpool express passed at something like 65mph. Note the lamp standing on the platform to the right, and the cable tray that connected to a telegraph pole on the same side. *Author's collection*

Above On Saturday 25 July 1959 'Princess Coronation' Class 'Pacific' No 46226 *Duchess of Norfolk* speeds W74, a Carlisle to Euston express, along the up main line towards Weaver Junction. Taken from just in front of the signal box, this view is looking roughly north in the direction of Preston Brook, Norton Crossing and Warrington. Had it been taken eight or nine years earlier, the boy sitting on the fence could well have been me. The elevated perch gave sufficient vision above the lineside shrubs to note all the relevant details. The point rodding in the foreground operated the crossover between the up and down main lines, while that running away from us from opposite the front of the engine operated the points for the refuge siding, which is obscured from view by the train. Just above the tender can be seen the top of two railway cottages; the one nearest the railway was the home of signalman Joe Huntbach and his family, the other occupied by a family called Horridge, not connected with the railway. Graham Bunn's home is hidden by trees just above the dome of the locomotive. *J. A. Peden*

Left Believe it or not, this is Birdswood, looking in the opposite direction on Thursday 15 July 1999 at the very spot where the Birdswood Up Home bracket signal was located. The only recognisable feature is the flyover under which the last part of this down Virgin express is passing at a speed in excess of 100mph. *Author*

lovely sunny afternoon, with the thudding of levers being released in the frame adding to the exciting railway atmosphere that seemed almost too good to be true. I wondered how Graham could live in such a wonderful place and not be affected by what was going on behind the railway fencing. Just imagine the thrill of seeing the clear profile of engine and coaches of an up Liverpool express as it thundered past the signal box high on the embankment right before our very eyes. Wonderful! What a discovery for us! A real treasure! I was already beginning to feel that this was my favourite spotting location. There would be times in the future when plans would be made to spend perhaps a full day here in the school summer holidays. We could even bring a tent. Yes, this was the place to be! Yet after hearing several trains pass by out of sight on the down Liverpool line, I began to feel that I was missing something. True, the engines going to Liverpool would likely have to come back along the up line sometime in the future, but we may not be here to see them, and what if they were ones we had not yet spotted? Something would have to be done to put that right. Little did I know just at that moment precisely how that dilemma would be solved and what it would lead to for Alan, Barrie and myself. But more of that in a later chapter. In the meanwhile our attention was completely centred on the several trains an hour – they were mainly passenger because of it being a Saturday afternoon – passing right before our very eyes, as well as noting the various signals that were visible to us and listening to the activities taking place within the elevated signal box. During the periods between the trains, we discussed our plans to cross the lines on our next visit to have a look at the down Liverpool line.

How very quickly that exciting afternoon passed. Before we even had time to become fully familiar with these new surroundings it was time to begin our trek back along the boat road to the Talbot Arms to catch the bus home. As it was our first visit to this railway paradise we decided to allow plenty of time for the walk back to the bus stop, leaving just after the Inverness-Euston train had sped through around 4.10pm. We found an alternative route for the first part of the walk, which took us alongside the railway fence towards Dutton Tunnel, then cut across the meadow to come out on the boat road near to the corner in the dip. As it happened, no trains came during the time we made this diversion, but it would be handy in future because it kept us within spotting distance for a longer period of time.

On reaching the Runcorn-Northwich road in the village, we stood at the bus stop opposite the Talbot Arms discussing the excitement of the afternoon. We soon realised that several villagers had appeared at intervals from behind a hedge near the bus stop, and on looking around the corner we saw a little Post Office store. There were still 10 minutes to wait for the bus, so in we went to see what was sold there. Naturally the Post Office part was closed, but it was obvious that a good selection of sweets and chocolate was available. An old lady, with her grey hair gathered into a bun, served us with our selected tube of wine gums, and we returned to the bus stop just in time to catch the red North Western double-decker bound for the Runcorn Transporter Bridge.

When I reached home at the end of the trip, Dad was in the back garden building his lily pond and Mum was – as I had hoped – in the kitchen preparing the evening meal, which, judging from the terrific smell permeating the kitchen, was just about ready to be served. Excellent timing, I thought.

'You look as if you've enjoyed your outing,' said Mum. 'Where did you say you were going?'

'Birdswood, not far from the Talbot Arms in Dutton,' I replied, and immediately launched into an enthusiastic report of our new-found trainspotting location as I began washing my grubby hands in the kitchen sink.

'How many times have I told you, Peter, not to wash your hands there when I'm cooking. If you can go all that way to get to your Birdswood, surely it's not too much trouble for you to go upstairs to the bathroom to wash your hands.'

'Sorry, Mum,' was my reply, but by that time I had completed the washing operation and was drying my hands on the kitchen towel. After such an eventful afternoon, no amount of 'ticking off' by my mother would have taken the edge off my enjoyment, and I began turning over in my mind all the things that had happened that day. What a truly wonderful day it had turned out to be, realistically much more than I had anticipated from what Graham had said. He had virtually staked his reputation on Birdswood meeting with our approval. There is no doubt that it had done that, and more besides. What an excellent spot to spend warm summer Saturday afternoons! The great mystery was how such a spot had not been picked out before now. At that time I became determined to improve my map-reading skills, because surely I should have seen that spot on the map where the two lines of railway joined.

My reverie was suddenly broken as I mentally focussed on Mum's remark, 'Anyway, never mind, it's done now. You are home just in time for tea, and I'm very glad you enjoyed yourself today.'

Enjoyed myself! That was an understatement, if ever I heard one!

6
SEE YOU IN COURT

Trainspotters are notorious for finding their way into places where they ought not to be in order to get a better view of passing trains, and even though it is sufficient simply to see and record the locomotive number, there is much more to it than that. Enthusiasts want to see and savour all the action, noting how the motion appears as an engine approaches, or watch with fascination the yawing action of a 'Crab' as it heads towards them. Sometimes you watch an approaching train and you just know that there is something different about its locomotive, without immediately being able to identify exactly what it is. Even a subtle change can have this effect on an observer, as I clearly remember from one particular occasion.

At Birdswood it was possible to get a more distant view of up trains by moving towards the up bracket signal rather than our usual place opposite the signal box, where some lineside bushes partially obstructed our view. One day we were sitting on the fence near the bracket signal, which was 'off' for an up train. The sound of the approaching train could be heard as it burst through the 84-yard-long Dutton Tunnel. Just before the tunnel the 1 in 180 uphill gradient from Preston Brook flattened off to a short level stretch as far as the up Liverpool flyover beside Birdswood box. To a powerful engine the uphill gradient presented no problem, so that on reaching this short level section of track most express trains were travelling around 70 miles an hour. The quite distinctive exhaust beat of a Stanier 'Princess Coronation' Class 'Pacific' could be heard. All eyes were trained on the point where the slight curve of the track emerged from the tunnel, to get the earliest possible glimpse of the hard-working engine at speed. Was it a 'semi', as we called those engines? Certainly the huge bulk of the front end gave that impression, but something didn't seem quite right. The 'Royal Scot' headboard was properly positioned on the top lamp bracket, but something looked different about this speeding giant. If it was a 'semi', it had been rebuilt to remove the sloping smokebox top, yet something in the area of the bottom of the smokebox seemed wrong, so perhaps it was something else. Yet what other locomotives running in this country had the massive appearance of those very powerful Stanier 'Pacifics'?

All these points were flashing through my mind as this train bore down on us at speed. Then it was near enough for the smokebox number to be spotted, and someone called out, '6233!'

So, sure enough it was a 'semi', but why did it not look right?

'*Duchess of Sutherland*!' yelled another boy as I confirmed the identity from the large cab-side number. By this time the locomotive was roaring past right in front of us, when suddenly the penny dropped for me.

'It's got no blinkers!' I shouted excitedly.

'Cor, yeah, look at that!' responded Alan with some astonishment.

It would be 1.10pm on Saturday 24 April 1954 as the photographer captured the down 'Royal Scot' speeding northwards past the Birdswood Down Starting signal at something like 75mph, powered by 'Princess Coronation' 'semi' No 46247 *City of Liverpool*. The matching set of Mark 1 coaches in 'plum and custard' livery sport the destination boards of this prestigious express, the locomotive having been cleaned for this turn of duty. Having left Euston at 10.05am and now approaching milepost 176 means that the average speed of just under 60mph has been maintained. *C. M. & J. M. Bentley*

No wonder the engine looked strange as it approached. I had never seen a 'semi' running without smoke-deflectors before, and it was simply this subtle difference that caused all of us so much consternation. Right away an argument broke out as to who had and who had not seen a Stanier 'Pacific' of the 'Princess Coronation' Class without its smoke deflectors before, and the subject was dropped only when – a couple of minutes later – the two almost brand-new diesel-electric locomotives Nos 10000 and 10001 powered a down Glasgow express at an impressive speed past the spot where we were sitting. Amidst all the furore nobody had noticed the down starter and Preston Brook slotted Distant quietly rise to the 'off' position.

All this goes to prove that there is much more to trainspotting than recording locomotive numbers, and in order to take the fullest possible advantage of any location, ways of getting a better view or methods of seeing more passing trains were always under review. At my favourite spot at Birdswood

The first two British main-line diesel-electric locomotives, Nos 10000 and 10001, are seen at Millers Dale station, near Buxton, in the summer of 1948. The 16-cylinder English Electric engine developed 1,600hp to drive the six nose-suspended motors, producing a tractive effort of 41,400lb. The weight was 121 tons 10 cwt, and only two were ever built. You can imagine the excitement I felt when I first saw 'the twins' later in 1948 at Birdswood as they hauled the 'Royal Scot' northwards along the West Coast Main Line at something like 80mph. Even before they appeared through the flyover the excitement began, because the sound was so unusual. Then when they appeared a few seconds later, that first impression was imprinted on my memory. Remember, the only diesel-electric locomotives around prior to these two were the 0-6-0 shunters (now Class 08) usually

seen at stations and in goods yards, pottering about at walking pace. *C. M. & J. M. Bentley*

there was a distinct disadvantage, which I shall explain later. This spot was a grassy clearing right beside the Up Main line just before it passed beneath the flyover carrying the up Liverpool line. A typical railway fence of stout creosoted uprights with three horizontal rails between ran from just opposite the signal box, alongside the up refuge siding all the way to Dutton Tunnel. The end of this wooden fence opposite the signal box provided a fine perch from which to observe passing trains. The section of track from there to the brick abutment of the flyover was bordered by a tensioned plain-wire fence. As the track was cut slightly into the ground in this area, there was a narrow strip of shallow embankment nurturing a sparse growth of shrubbery, which, fortunately, was not high enough to obscure our view of traffic. Behind the fence was an almost triangular-shaped clearing, fairly flat but with one or two minor undulations, covered in lovely unspoiled turf. Unspoiled, that is, by the pats left behind by grazing cattle, so it was perfect for playing football, cricket or any other such pastime between the all-important trains. Alongside this clearing, away from the tracks, was a wooded area that sloped down to the Trent & Mersey Canal where a lock-keeper's cottage, a set of locks, a small dry-dock for the repair of narrowboats and a sluice provided occasional interest when things on the railway were quieter than usual.

So with all these assets, what could possibly be viewed as a disadvantage? Simply this. From that idyllic location it was impossible to see any traffic on the down Liverpool line, because it lay out of sight on the far side of the up Liverpool line, which was carried on an embankment at high level to a flyover crossing both tracks of the main line. Birdswood signal box stood at this high spot alongside the up Liverpool line. To some it might seem irrelevant that a few of the trains could not be seen, because of the profusion of very interesting trains on the main line, but knowing full well that almost all of the Liverpool expresses were hauled by equally interesting and powerful engines as those trains on the West Coast Main Line, we did not want to miss out on a single one. It is true

to say that the Stanier 'Pacifics' were mostly of the 'Princess Royal' Class on the Liverpool trains, whereas the Scottish expresses were powered by 'Princess Coronation' locomotives, but both routes enjoyed a goodly number of 'Royal Scot', 'Jubilee' and 'Patriot' Class engines as well as 'Pacifics'. You may, then, begin to understand our pressing need to see whatever passed along that obscured down Liverpool line.

How could such a problem be overcome? Could we all scramble up the tree-covered embankment adjacent to the flyover? Yes, but the signalman would then have easily seen us trespassing and would have shouted to us to get back behind the fence. What about climbing to the top of one of the trees in the wood? While that would give a good observation point, it would certainly be uncomfortable for more than a few minutes. Whichever one of us was drawn to act as the observer would have to rely solely on his pals to record all the numbers for him, for the simple reason that he would be too busy hanging on for dear life to be able to use his hands for anything so simple as writing numbers in a notebook. No, there just had to be a better solution to this pressing and important problem, but what was it?

After some strategic planning had been thrashed out and all the available options considered, a large black cloud of despair seemed to descend upon us all. Sentenced to being restricted to the main-line traffic and the up Liverpool trains only, we began to accept the inevitability of the situation when our school pal Graham Bunn, who, you will recall, lived in the cottage adjacent to the end of the canal tunnel and who, at that very moment, had joined our little group in the clearing opposite the signal box, said, 'Why don't you use the public footpath to cross the lines into Birdswood? You could sit on the fence at the edge of the wood and you'll be able to see all the trains.'

'What a brilliant idea, Bunny,' said Barrie, patting Graham on the back so hard that he almost collapsed under the barrage.

'Why didn't we think of that before?' asked Alan, who now sported an extra-wide grin. At this point I remembered that Graham had told

Photographed from the public footpath leading diagonally up the embankment to the signal box, 'Royal Scot' Class No 46140 *The King's Royal Rifle Corps* hauls a Class H up freight along the West Coast Main Line towards Weaver Junction on Saturday 24 April 1954. This was a Crewe North engine, which would normally have been working express passenger trains, but could have been rostered on a running-in turn after overhaul at Crewe Works. The washing visible through the trees on the right is in the garden of Graham Bunn's cottage, but what is not shown between the washing and the railway fence is a shallow valley through which the Trent & Mersey Canal approaches its tunnel just in front of the Bunns' cottage and running for about a mile towards Preston Brook. *C. M. & J. M. Bentley*

us of this public footpath when we first came to Birdswood.

'That's a super idea, Graham. Let's go now!' I said, looking around for my haversack.

'I've got something to do at home,' said Graham determinedly.

Here I should explain that the haversack carried by men and boys in those early days after the Second World War was in fact a gas-mask case, a semi-rigid bag about 9 by 7 by 3 inches, with an adjustable strap that was usually passed over the head and worn diagonally across the upper body so that the bag hung around waist level. It was well made of khaki-coloured linen which must have been reinforced with some form of stiffening, and had a flap over the top that could be fastened with two brass press-studs. They were readily obtainable at the army surplus stores and were used by workmen to carry their lunch to work. There were many other uses to which these versatile bags were put, including that described here. But back to my story.

The three of us collected up our lunch bags, coats, *ABCs* and notebooks and walked with Graham to the point in the wooden fence where the public footpath crossed. There was no stile, but the fencing was firm and easily climbed. The public footpath skirted the siding to a point where it joined the main running line, then crossed the two main line tracks at right angles before mounting a wooden step at the foot of the far embankment; through this step ran signal wires from the signal box to the Down Starter and Up Distant and Home signals. The footpath then followed a rising course diagonally to the left up the embankment towards the signal box at the top. After passing the foot of the steps to the signal box, it crossed the up Liverpool line squarely by the box, then ran right alongside the line for some 30 yards before dropping diagonally down the other side of the embankment towards the down Liverpool line. Once over the line, the path crossed a similar wooden railway fence and disappeared into Birds Wood.

Clearly our observation point was to be atop this fence at the point where the public footpath crossed. The excitement of having solved the problem was boosted soon after our arrival at this new-found spot by a down Liverpool express hauled by 'Princess Royal'

Above On Saturday 23 July 1955 most of the signal box's sliding windows are letting in plenty of fresh air as No 46256 *Sir William A. Stanier FRS* – named after its designer – passes at speed with an up express for Euston. This photograph, taken from the down Liverpool line, shows the elevated position of Birdswood signal box on the embankment alongside the up Liverpool line. A public footpath crossed the line precisely where the front of the engine is passing. It then continued on this side of the track for a few yards before coming down the embankment diagonally to a position to the right of the photographer, where it crossed the down Liverpool track into Birds Wood itself. An express such as this one passing so close to the box would fairly make the windows rattle. *J. A. Peden*

Below A 1960 view along the down Liverpool track as it climbs away from the main line at 1 in 151, showing clearly the difference in level compared to the up Liverpool track running over the flyover. The down Liverpool Home signal, with its tall repeater on the wrong side of the track, stands close to the point where the public footpath crosses the fence into Birds Wood on the left. *R. Stephens*

Class No 46208 *Princess Helena Victoria*. For me this was a 'cop' and made the effort of changing location well worthwhile, but it wasn't very long before we came to realise that this spot, too, had a rather annoying disadvantage.

Because we were now on the west side of the tracks, the main-line tracks were visible only from the flyover southwards (that is, way over to our right) and speeding southbound expresses seemed to shoot through the flyover and away before we could see their numbers. As well as the speed, there was the great disadvantage of only having the cab-side number to see, so that if an engine was fairly dirty, sometimes even that number was not so clear. How were we to get around this new-found problem? Well, some of the difficulty could be alleviated if we walked on the grass verge alongside the track, yet keeping well clear of it. Admittedly this was away from the footpath, but it did give us a better chance of observing the traffic on the main line.

Unknown to us there was a relief signalman on duty that afternoon who must have been watching us stray from the public right of way and go alongside the track. We became aware of his vigilance when we heard a voice boom out through a megaphone, 'Get back on the path!'

This relief signalman I later learned was a Mr Chetwynd, who was usually called to Birdswood duty when one of the regular signalmen was on leave. Whether he knew that the law allowed the public only to 'pass and repass' along a public footpath rather than encamp upon it as we did, or that he felt concerned for our safety as we walked along the grass beside the track, I do not know, but he was obviously unhappy with what we were doing. We complied immediately with his demand and went back to our perch on the fence beside the wood and made the best of a bad job.

After about half an hour we had had enough of this restricted site and decided to forfeit the chance of noting all engines on the down Liverpool line, preferring our original location on the grassy clearing. So we retraced our steps along the public footpath, crossed over the up Liverpool line, past the signal box

steps and down the embankment to cross the main lines back to the fence beside the bracket signal. But boy! What a surprise awaited us as we climbed the fence. Two burly policemen were waiting, their patrol car in the background near the canal tunnel. I thought my time had come, as I had always harboured a dread of being carted off in a police vehicle (I think this must have been the result of some threat my mother had made in the past when I was misbehaving) to be imprisoned in some dank, dark cell at the police station. The policemen had just climbed the path from where their car was parked, and had passed through the gate onto the narrow strip of grassland that belonged to the uncle of the girl who later became my wife. It was abundantly clear that we were the focus of both policemen's rapt attention, confirmed by what I felt was the slightly sarcastic question voiced by one of them. 'And where do you think you've been, then?'

Notebook already in hand, he called us to him and began to question us about our trip over the lines. In fairness to them both, they were only responding, apparently, to a call from the relief signalman via 'Control' because we had not stuck to the path. We explained that yes, we had strayed from the path, but had returned to it after the signalman had shouted at us and had not gone off it after that. It seems that the police had been told that we were continually wandering alongside the track off the public right of way, and that the signalman was concerned for our safety. All our particulars were noted down in the pocketbook held at the ready by one of the policemen, after which a stern warning was given not to do it again. Imagine the relief we all felt when the notebook was returned to the policeman's breast pocket and he and his colleague turned to go back to their black Rover.

A sense of nausea engulfed us all as we wondered what we should do next.

'Let's go home,' said Alan, looking at his watch.

Noting the time, Barrie said: 'The bus isn't due for more than an hour yet.'

The 2-hourly service operated by the North Western Road Car Company between

Northwich and Runcorn passed through Dutton village at 4.40pm, but it would take us about 10 minutes – if we didn't dawdle – to walk along the boat road that led from the canal tunnel entrance and meandered through some meadows to the village. As already mentioned, so as not to miss any trains as we walked to the bus stop outside the Post Office opposite the Talbot Arms public house, we would sometimes take the route through two meadows as an alternative to the boat road because we could walk alongside the railway fence until we almost reached the village. Then we would hope we could make the short transition from the railway fence across the field to a point further up the boat road without being spotted by the farmer, Fred Hazlehurst, my future wife's uncle.

As we had almost an hour to spare before the bus was due, we decided to go to the Post Office shop to buy a penny apple from old Granny Hazlehurst, the lady with her hair in a bun. These apples were grown in her orchard and were most delicious. I'm sure she would sort out the largest ones for us, because they would usually last a lot longer than the 10-minute bus trip to Halton and in our eyes represented value for money. And unless we had spotted an engine not previously seen, or some unusual form of rail traffic had passed during our visit to Birdswood, these huge penny apples were the icing on the cake of our afternoon outing. However, we would not have been so satisfied had we had only the icing!

On the way home we decided it would be best to tell our parents right away of our brush with the law, as we felt we had not done anything to warrant any restrictive or punishing consequences. How strange it is that parents sometimes don't need to ask if anything is wrong – they can tell from your face! When I opened the back door and walked into the kitchen, Mum was there preparing our evening meal. As she turned to greet me, instead of the usual, 'Hello, have you had a nice time?' she raised both eyebrows and asked, 'What have you been up to?'

Here I should explain that this was in 1950, on Saturday 18 February to be exact, long before we had a telephone installed, so unless the policemen had called at my home on their way back to Runcorn Police Station, there was no way my mother could have been informed of our escapade. Was it a loving mother's intuitive instinct that her offspring had experienced a spot of bother? Or was it the offspring's countenance, affected by that confrontation with the law of the land? Whatever the answer, Mum seemed to know that things had not gone well that afternoon. So, having hung up my school blazer on the hook under the stairs, dumped my now empty lunch bag on the floor in the corner of the kitchen and placed my ABC and notebook carefully on the sideboard in the dining room, I stood by the kitchen door and told Mum all about the episode with the police.

'And are you sure you didn't leave the footpath again after the signalman had shouted at you?' she enquired, in what I felt was a very understanding way and with a rather trusting and sympathetic look in her eye.

'No, Mum, honest we didn't. There's glass all round that signal box and he would have seen us if we'd done it again.'

'All right, I believe you, Peter,' she said, 'but you'll have to tell your father when he gets back from the barbers.'

Every other Saturday afternoon Dad visited Harry Peacock's barber shop in Runcorn for his usual short back and sides, and as it was now around 5 o'clock he was due home any minute. I remember thinking, 'I wish he would hurry up, then I could get it all over with at one go.' If Runcorn were at home playing one of their Cheshire League opponents, he would be home any minute, because on those Saturdays few men would visit the barber for a haircut, preferring to watch their local football team play on the Canal Street ground. Just a few minutes later I heard Dad's Austin 10 pull up on the short drive outside the house. I got it over with right away, telling him honestly all the facts as they had occurred. After listening quietly – and I hoped sympathetically – he then asked me a question.

'Do you know why that signalman probably called the police?'

'No,' I replied, 'because we went back to the path as soon as he shouted at us.'

'Yes, I believe you,' Dad said, 'but he was

probably worried in case you strayed onto the track and an express came speeding round the corner and hit you. You could have been killed.'

'But Dad, we were not on the track, we were on the grass at the side of the line. Anyway, if a train was due we'd have seen the Home signal up. Honestly, Dad, we were not playing dangerously.'

As a boy I was no angel, and I knew I couldn't pull the wool over my father's eyes. Barrie and Alan felt the same about their parents, which is why we agreed to come clean with them. Now I had told my parents the truth, I somehow knew they believed me and felt glad inside that this bond of trust seemed to make itself felt on this occasion.

'Well, don't worry yourself about it, but make sure you don't do anything like that again,' Dad warned.

Now that was over, I felt that I could divert my attention to much more important matters, so after the meal I went to my room and underscored the engines I had seen that day for the first time – only three, but they had to be neatly marked off in the ABC. By the way, although spotters usually carried their ABC with them, they would not usually mark off the engines seen until it could be done properly at home. Imagine the mess that could be made of such an important book if the underlining was done – as some did it – in the standing position on an embankment or the station platform.

Many weeks passed and the school spring holidays started. Two blissful weeks of not having to go to school – everyone knows how good that feels, especially when there are interesting things with which to fill all those lengthening spring days. I recall feeling that the holidays could go on for ever, because we always had something interesting to do with our time, including some serious mid-week trainspotting. Please don't think, however, that we had no other interests. Far from it – we were forever thinking up some project or other to fill our days, such as fabricating a 'flying saucer' from a hoop covered with sacking and launching it from the top of Halton Castle over a small group of unsuspecting villagers walking along Main Street. The shock on

their faces as they looked into the sky on hearing our loud shouts of 'Flying saucer!' is something to remember with amusement, especially one old lady who, on seeing our contraption floating through the sky over this quiet country village, dropped her shopping basket and ran into Rathbone's butchers shop to seek shelter, leaving her cabbage and onions rolling down the main road. Such escapades not only kept us occupied, but also blanked from our memories the episode that ended with our confrontation with the police at Birdswood. Then one day it happened!

Any mail for Dad was propped up on the mantelpiece so he could see it as soon as he stepped into the dining room. I had not paid any attention to the large brown envelope with the official crest on the back as I had picked up the mail from the hall floor after the morning visit of the postman, but when Dad got home that evening I soon knew all about its contents.

'It's a summons for you to appear in court, Peter,' said Dad with a trace of a smile on his face. 'It seems your escapades have caught up with you. We have to appear at the Runcorn Juvenile Court on Wednesday 12 April at 10.00am to face a charge of trespassing on railway property.'

My heart sank, and felt as though it was bumping along the bottom of the ocean. Court? Trespassing? Oh, yes, I remember that day, and it all came flooding back to me. Dad looked me straight in the eye and said, 'We'll have to face the music, son.'

It was not very often he called me 'son', preferring to use my name, but it seemed to me at that very moment that he used the expression 'son' only because difficulties lay ahead. But how very reassuring it was that he'd said, 'We'll have to face the music.' So he was going to support me. Good. What transpired after that in my discussion with Dad I cannot recall, but I do remember dashing off to Barrie's house to see if he'd had a similar experience that day. Oh, yes, he certainly had. Thankfully his father was equally supportive. We left his home to pop down the road to Alan's, where no doubt the brown envelope had rippled the pond, but there was no one at home.

NUMBER	NAME OF INFORMANT. COMPLAINANT OR APPLICANT	NAME OF CHILD OR YOUNG PERSON AND IN CASE OF COMPLAINTS UNDER SECT. 44, 45 OR 54, OF THE EDUCATION ACT, 1921, THE NAME OF THE PARENT OR GUARDIAN	AGE	NATURE OF OFFENCE." MATTER OF COMPLAINT OR GROUND OF APPLICATION	DATE (OF OFFENCE ETC.)

50 IN THE *County* OF *Chester* REGISTER OF THE JUVENILE COURT SITTING AT
PETTY SESSIONAL DIVISION OF *Runcorn* *THE OFFENCE OF WHICH THE CHILD OR YOUNG PERSON IS FOUND GUILTY SHOULD BE CLEARLY STATED.

12th April 1950 — Before :- E.S. Lea Esq. and Mrs. Broadhurst.

1	British Railways			Trespassing on the Railway at Aston Cheshire the property of the British Transport Commission	1950 February
2	"			Do.	"
3	"			Do.	"
4	"			Do.	"
5	"	Peter Haddock	13	Do.	"
6	"			Do.	"
7	"			Do.	"
8	"			Do.	"

Above and right Pages recording the sitting of the Runcorn Juvenile Court held on Wednesday 12 April 1950, presided over by magistrates E. S. Lea Esquire and Mrs Broadhurst. The offence was 'Trespassing on the Railway at Aston Cheshire the property of the British Transport Commission' and occurred on Saturday 18 February 1950. After the pleas of 'Guilty' had been entered, the adjudication reads 'Discharged absolutely on payment of 4/- Court costs and 9d witness fee'. *Author's collection*

Barrie and I decided to go for a walk up the castle, so we climbed the hill opposite the top of Holly Bank Road, up what we called the 'elephant steps' beside Stimson's large detached home and huge garden, then higher still across the grassy bank leading up to the western end of the Hill School, over the stone stile in the sandstone wall and up onto the plateau alongside the base of the castle wall. By the way, the term 'elephant steps' was used to differentiate them from the much narrower and steeper 'monkey steps', which were cut from solid sandstone and gave access from Main Street beside Dicky Done's newsagents shop to the flat area outside the main door of St Mary's church.

Much of our youthful adventure took place in and around Halton Castle, built in 1072 by Hugh Lupus and ruined in 1643 by Oliver Cromwell. This lovely ruined castle sat on the knoll at the north end of the Cheshire Plain, overlooking Runcorn, the River Mersey and Widnes, with wide ranging views far afield. It was said that on a clear day one could see six counties from this hilltop. Lancashire lay only a few miles away to the north just across the River Mersey, Widnes being the nearest Lancashire town – though it is now officially in Cheshire – and Liverpool Cathedral tower could be seen on the distant skyline. Looking in a roughly easterly direction the outskirts of Warrington could be discerned. Further round to the east the Pennines were visible, with Mow Cop in Staffordshire on the southern skyline. Perhaps the most dominating feature was the profile of the man's face of Helsby Hill, beyond which the blue line of the Welsh mountains along the Flintshire coast were often clearly to be seen. From this elevated position it was possible to keep an eye on any rail traffic running on the Liverpool branch, which ran along the top of an embankment from Sutton Weaver northwards to the point where it ran into a cutting just before reaching the overbridge at Lodge Lane and then Halton Junction. Many is the time we could have added to the list of 'cops' if we had been able to get our hands on a powerful telescope, but they were few and far between in those days.

Today, though, the only youthful activity we took part in near the castle was a solemn stroll around the perimeter path, during which we discussed the possible outcome of our appearance in court and what effect, if any, it would have on our reputations in the village. It was really serious stuff, not to be shrugged off as of no importance. How could an

50

Runcorn	THE	DAY OF	19

IF IT IS NOT THE OFFENCE ENTERED IN COLUMN 5, PARTICULARS SHOULD BE GIVEN IN COLUMN 9.

R.R.47. SHAW & SONS LTD., FETTER LANE, E.C., 70, 61060 (v)

DATE WHEN TAKEN TO PLACE OF SAFETY 7	PLEA (OFFENCE) 8	MINUTE OF ADJUDICATION* 9	TIME ALLOWED FOR PAYMENT AND INSTALMENTS OF FINES 10	SIGNATURES OF JUSTICES 11
	Guilty	Discharged absolutely on payment of 4/- Court costs and 9d witness fee	Paid	E.S. Lea
	Guilty	Do	Paid	E.S. Lea
	Guilty	Do	Paid	E.S. Lea
	Guilty	Do	Paid	E.S. Lea
	Guilty	Do	Paid	E.S. Lea
	Guilty	Do	Paid	E.S. Lea
	Guilty	Do	Paid	E.S. Lea
	Guilty	Do	Paid	E.S. Lea

innocent afternoon of trainspotting land us all in the juvenile court?

I don't recall any of our worries revolving around a Borstal term, as none of us thought the matter to be that serious, but we knew it could have long-term financial implications as far as our pocket money was concerned, and if that did transpire, gone would be any plans for outings to places like Crewe or Liverpool Lime Street on trainspotting expeditions.

The dawn of Wednesday 12 April 1950 arrived, and I recall that the only positive thought that passed through my mind on waking was that I wouldn't have to go to school that morning. The proceedings were to be held in the courtroom adjoining the Police Station at the bottom of Bridge Street and High Street in Runcorn. The bus stop was right outside the Police Station, and my trepidation began in earnest as we three boys followed Mrs Looker, Mr Dunbebin and my father up the steps into that building. I remember very little if anything of the proceedings – perhaps obliterated from my memory by such a solemn occasion – but the awesomeness of that panelled courtroom, the wooden benches and many officials has stayed with me to this day.

During the course of my research in the preparation of this book I made a visit to the Cheshire County Record Office at Chester where, in the record book of proceedings for the Runcorn Juvenile Court, I was able to trace the actual entry relative to my appearance. The magistrates were E. S. Lea Esq and Mrs Broadhurst. The nature of the offence was noted as 'Trespassing on the Railway at Aston Cheshire the property of the British Transport Commission'. We all pleaded guilty, and the record shows in the adjudication column that we were 'Discharged absolutely on payment of 4/- Court costs and 9d witness fee.'

We were asked by the magistrate if we had wandered off the public footpath on the day in question, to which we gave an affirmative reply. When he asked if we trespassed on the railway again after the signalman had shouted to us to get back to the footpath, we honestly replied that we had not, which – I thought – impressed him. He then mumbled something to the effect that 'this case should not have been brought' and dismissed it, with the direction that the costs of the signalman, Mr Chetwynd – having lost a day's pay to attend court – should be borne by our respective parents.

Accordingly our parents each had to pay the 4s 9d. The outcome could have been very much worse if the presiding magistrate had ordered that we never go on or near railway property again. That would have been the trainspotters' equivalent of being given a sentence of life imprisonment! Mercifully for us we were not subjected to any such stipulation.

Since that time I have often wondered if that magistrate – in his younger days – had been a trainspotter himself.

7
BIRDSWOOD SIGNAL BOX

It was following a bicycle trip to Birdswood in the summer of 1951 that one of my most exciting schoolboy dreams was realised. On that particular occasion only Alan Looker and myself had decided to spend the Saturday afternoon doing some serious trainspotting and hàd, at the last minute, made the arrangements to cycle to Dutton so as to save the bus fare of fourpence each return. There was a lot that could be done with fourpence in those days, and anyway the cycle ride to Dutton was a pleasant one. The big advantage of cycling – in addition to the financial saving – was that the lengthy walk from the bus stop at the Talbot Arms in Dutton village down the boat road to Birdswood was eliminated. Despite the rough surface of this track, which meant that a careful look-out had to be kept to prevent puncturing the tyres or even buckling a wheel, having a bike meant that we could, if we wished, stay on longer beside the railway tracks if the traffic seemed interesting.

It had become our usual practice to ride down the boat road as far as the stock-proof gate in the fence near to Graham Bunn's home and leave our bikes just to the side of the gate clear of the path. Then we would walk through the gate and along through the narrow meadow to our favourite spot just opposite the signal box. On the grassy clearing there we could play football, cricket or other games while waiting for the trains to go by, and I recall that an iron post (which I later learned was a LNWR boundary post) was conveniently positioned to be useful as a

wicket. Why that post was there I never did discover, but it seemed rather odd that it should be some few yards away from the stout wooden fence bordering the track. Anyway, we often used it as a wicket in the cricket season, and during football games it became one side of the goal, with a pile of jackets and raincoats making the other post.

However, that day Alan and I decided that we would just sit on the wooden fencing, where we discussed the different engines that we hoped to 'cop' and some of the more interesting ones we had recently seen. It is quite surprising how two boys who spent a good deal of time locospotting together could have such a difference in engines underlined in their ABCs. It could easily become the subject of a lengthy argument if one of us, while out alone, spotted a locomotive that was sought after by the others. One such example of this involved my above-mentioned sighting of the streamlined No 6227 *Duchess of Devonshire* (or was it No 6224 *Princess Alexandra?*). Between trains on this beautifully sunny and warm afternoon such a discussion helped while away the time until the next train passed. If one had a newer *ABC* than the other, the time could be usefully spent comparing the differences that came about as a result of new engines entering service or older ones being scrapped. All the time this was going on, we were aware of the sound of bell codes ringing out and levers thumping in the frame of the signal box as the duty signalman went about his work. Most of the sliding windows of the box were open, and occasionally we would catch sight of the signalman as he came to the window when trains passed by.

It was during a short lull between trains on that afternoon that the signalman came to the window on our side of the box and shouted down to us, 'Have either of you lads got a bike?'

His voice carried down to us quite well on this lovely summer day.

'We've both got one,' I shouted back, wondering why he should ask such a question. The mystery was quickly resolved when he said, 'Would you be able to run an errand for me on your bike, please, to help me out of a jam?'

'Yes, what is it?' I asked.

'Can you come up to the box and I'll tell you? It is quite safe to cross the lines now, so come up this path here,' he said, pointing to a cinder path that started on his side of the line just opposite our 'perch' on the fence and climbed steeply up the bank towards the bottom of the signal box steps.

He had hardly finished uttering the words before we were both down off that fence in a flash and crossing the main lines towards a wooden step at the base of the embankment. I have no idea what Alan was thinking, because we never discussed it later, but my mind was racing at the thought of actually going inside the signal box, which I saw as one of the railway nerve-centres.

'I wonder if he'll invite us up into the box?' My rather hopeful question was put to Alan as we climbed the steep path.

'We'll soon know,' was his reasoned and logical reply, the tone of which was more sceptical than expectant. 'But he did say he wanted us to go somewhere for him, so I don't expect we'll get inside.'

We were both quite out of breath after climbing up that embankment at great pace, and when we reached the bottom of the signal box steps the signalman was standing at the door with a smile on his face awaiting our arrival. An elderly man with white hair and a jovial face, he was wearing black trousers, which I noticed were nicely pressed with sharp creases and looked very smart, unlike so many

This is the view we had from our favourite location where we sat on the fence. Mr Culshaw appeared at the window on the extreme left when he first invited us inside. The booking desk and telephones are located behind the other set of windows on the right in this elevation. *Author's collection*

railwaymen I had seen, and his white shirt had the sleeves rolled up to the elbows. Despite the warmth of the weather, he still wore a collar and tie, though not the typical railway waistcoat I had seen other railwaymen wearing.

'Come up and I'll tell you what I want you to do,' he said cheerfully, beckoning us up the many steps into the box.

I felt so excited at the prospect that I wanted to bound up the steps two at a time. The straight flight of wooden steps had a stout handrail on each side and felt solid as we climbed up to the small platform that acted as a landing for the outward-opening signal box door. Amidst the excitement my mind was taking in many of the little details of this new experience, but the thing that stands out in my memory to this day was the signal box floor. As I approached the top of the steps and looked in through the door, I could see what seemed like a vast expanse of clean, shiny light-brown linoleum. Why this fact should form such a strong memory I do not know, but perhaps it was because I was half expecting the floor to be plain wooden boards. Not only that, but I must have expected them to be dirty too, because of the cinder path. As it was, that clean shiny floor seemed to glow in the strong afternoon sunlight and make the box most welcoming.

Inside the box there seemed to be so much to see, with a long row of brightly coloured levers with polished handles, the block shelf with its various instruments and bells, and the stand-up desk with the typical railway clock above it. But the overall first impression of being in that 'inner sanctum' of railway operations was one of bright cleanliness. This was likely due to the fact that the sides of the signal box were almost entirely of glass, together with the fact that obviously this signalman cared for the place where he spent about a third of his life. I felt as if I had just stepped into Aladdin's cave, there were so many 'treasures' to be seen, and I could have stood there for hours just staring at everything with immense pleasure had it not been for the voice of the signalman:

'Sit down on that locker, and I'll tell you what I want you to do for me.'

We both sat on a wooden box beside a black cast-iron stove while he sat on a similar box on the other side of the stove. I did notice that on his box there were some cushions from an old armchair, which obviously made it a much

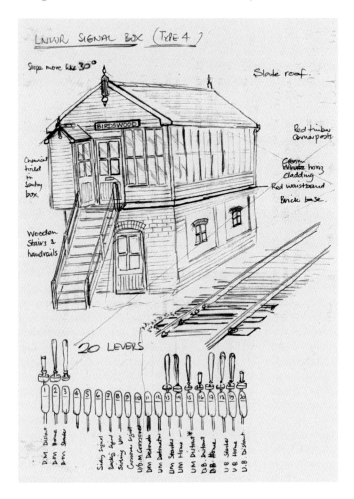

My original sketch of Birdswood signal box, drawn entirely from memory some 40 years after my last visit to the box. It was the beginning of a long process of trawling from my memory as much detail as I possibly could about the signal box, with the intention of making a scale model of it. However, the more details I recalled the more I began to formulate the idea of writing down all the experiences I had enjoyed, centred on this lovely signal box. *Author*

more comfortable seat for the signalman on duty.

'My name is George Culshaw, and I live at Preston-on-the-Hill, near Preston Brook. I've left my baggin at home and wonder if you could go there on your bikes and get it for me, otherwise I'll have nothing to eat until I get home after 10 o'clock tonight, and that will never do!' 'Baggin' was a Cheshire expression for a snack meal such as a sandwich, prepared at home and taken to work to be eaten whenever there was an appropriate moment.

Ah! So that's why he wanted to know if we had a bike, because Preston-on-the-Hill was about 2 miles away.

'Yes, we can go, can't we Alan?' I said, speaking for us both and hoping that Alan would agree and not want to take unfair advantage by suggesting that I went alone and he stay in the signal box.

'Yes,' he replied. 'It shouldn't take us long to get there and back. Which house in the village do you live at, Mr Culshaw?'

'Ivy Dene. It's on the right hand side on the corner just before you turn down the lane for Hatton. You can't miss it. I expect the wife will have discovered I've left my food behind and is wondering how she can get it to me.'

'OK, we'll go and get it for you,' I said, standing up ready to leave. Though not wishing to leave this interesting place, my mind was racing ahead and I was already thinking of what would happen when we got back with Mr Culshaw's food. He would probably invite us to stay in the signal box with him, I reasoned hopefully to myself.

'While you're gone I'll keep a note of all the engines that pass by, so that you'll not miss any.'

'That's no good,' responded Alan. 'We've got to see them ourselves before we can underline them in our ABC.'

Just as he said that, a deep loud bell rang out four quick beats. Mr Culshaw immediately went to the shelf over the levers and tapped something out on one of the lovely wooden-boxed instruments, then turned a black knob, which seemed to move one of two needles on the instrument. Turning to us he said, 'It's the 2 o'clock Euston express from Liverpool Lime Street.'

A life-long railwayman, Mr Culshaw was well known in the area for his cheerful disposition, as well as being a signalman extraordinaire. As a result of a wound sustained while on active service in France during the First World War, his left arm was 5 inches shorter than his right, but that in no way detracted from his ability to do his work. *Author's collection*

Right away he tapped out what seemed like the same code on the next instrument, then went on to say, 'I'll be with you in just a minute.'

Almost before he had finished speaking, another bell sounded out four rings, but this time the bell was a rather deeper tone and sounded quite mellow. Mr Culshaw looked towards the second instrument and I noticed one of the needles flick from the vertical position to an angle. He then went to the door end of the row of levers and pulled the red one next to the end so that it stuck out into the room, not quite obstructing the way to the door. It had a small cast-iron plate screwed to the front of the lever stem just below the handle, and on it the number 19 was picked out in white paint. He then pulled the next red one, 18, in the same manner.

What happened next took me completely by surprise. I was sitting nearer to Mr Culshaw than was Alan. Looking at me and pointing to the last lever in the row, a yellow one numbered 20, which had a shorter handle than the other two, Mr Culshaw said, 'Here, you can pull this one off. It's an easy one, so you don't need to pull very hard.'

I leaped towards the lever, hardly able to believe what he had said, and tried to move it in much the same way as he had pulled the other two. It came back so easily that I could have done it with one hand. I felt so pleased with myself at having been involved in clearing the road for the passage of the express, but when I looked in Alan's direction I was not sure how he was feeling at that moment. I only know that if he had pulled the lever while I watched, I would certainly have felt a bit jealous.

Feeling slightly guilty about my privilege, I stepped over to Alan and, changing the subject, said, 'About that list of numbers Mr Culshaw said he'd make for us – don't you think it would be a good idea if he did that, then we'd know what we've missed?' As Alan nodded I turned to the signalman and continued, 'So it would be a help if you could take the numbers for us please, Mr Culshaw.'

'I'll do that,' he said, 'and just before you go, tell me your names, just in case anyone comes looking for you.'

Having told him who we were, we made our way out of the signal box. As we were descending the steps he pointed toward the Up Main Home signal and said, 'Take that path that heads for the end of the siding. That's the public footpath – you'll be safe crossing there just now. The train we're expecting will come down this line up here next to the box. I'll look forward to seeing you in about half an hour or so.'

By that time we were off the signal box steps and had turned onto another rather longer cinder path that led diagonally down the embankment. It was not as steep as the one we had climbed to get to the box. Just before we came to the point where the path crossed the tracks of the West Coast Main Line, I heard two beats on the first bell and – even though I did not yet know that the bell code meant 'Train Entering Section' – wondered just how much longer it would be before the express from Lime Street appeared. We crossed the down and up main lines and walked around the head of the siding, then alongside it for 50 yards or so before climbing the fence into the narrow meadow. By now we were very close to the Up Main Home signal and not far from where we had left our bikes.

Alan must have been quietly thinking about pulling some levers himself, because he then broke the silence by saying, 'I wonder if he'll let us stay in the signal box when we get back with his food.'

'That would be smashing if he would,' I replied, 'but somehow I don't think we'd be allowed in there, do you?' What an unreasonable comment in view of what we had just experienced!

'We can ask him, though,' retorted Alan. 'You never know. Anyway, what was it like pulling that little lever?'

'Easy,' I said, trying not to make too much of it in case Alan really was jealous, 'but it didn't feel as if there was any signal wire attached to it. I'll ask him about that when we get back.'

By that time we had reached our bicycles and began pedalling up the boat road away from the railway, but we had gone no further than the top of the first short incline when we heard the distinctive sound of an express train travelling at high speed. Stopping and looking back towards the signal box, we saw a lovely clean 'Princess Royal' appear from behind the trees lining the track, speeding its way towards Weaver Junction, Crewe and Euston, hauling a very long train. We were too far away to take the engine number, but reassured each other that Mr Culshaw would note it for us. We could quite legitimately underline it in our ABC if we hadn't seen it before. Anyway, we would have to wait until we returned to the signal box before we would know which engine it was. There were only two engines of that class I had not yet seen, so I was secretly hoping it was either No 46204 Princess Louise or No 46211 Queen Maud so that I could add it to my collection.

Our rough ride of about half a mile along the boat road brought us to the A533 at the Talbot Arms, where we turned right to pedal along the main road for about 500 yards. Then, turning sharp left at what used to be the old workhouse (which then was a geriatric hospital but is now demolished with new houses built on the site), we entered a country lane leading through some lovely countryside to Preston-on-the-Hill about a mile away.

Although for both of us this was fresh cycling territory, we had no difficulty finding Ivy Dene, set at the corner of Hatton Lane. Leaving our bikes leaning on one pedal against the kerbstones, we opened the garden gate and walked up the path to the front door. I noticed that the garden was beautifully kept with a small lawn bordered by flowers on either side of the path. As the name of the cottage implied, there was much ivy growing around the front door in typical 'chocolate-box' style, though this was a red-brick semi-detached house that looked as if it belonged to one of the local country estates. It was not built in a style typical of the railway cottages that were to be seen in various parts of Cheshire.

Knocking at the front door, I began to wonder what sort of lady Mrs Culshaw would be and how she would respond to our errand. I need not have worried. The front door opened and there stood a small, white-haired lady looking slightly puzzled at seeing two unknown schoolboys standing on her doorstep. She was neatly dressed in a flowered frock, most of which was covered with a crisp white pinafore, and I noticed that her hands were dusted with white powder. As I had many times seen my own mother in that situation, I concluded that she was busy baking. Before she could ask us what we wanted, I blurted out, 'Mr Culshaw sent us to…'

'Oh, I know,' she interrupted, breaking into a broad smile, 'to collect his food that he left behind when he went to work in a hurry this afternoon. You'd better come in for a minute while I put it in a bag for you.' Then, after holding open the door as we entered, she continued, 'I've just made some scones – would you like one with a cup of tea, or would you rather have pop?'

'Pop would be very nice,' replied Alan, as I began to realise the source of the lovely smell that drifted into my nostrils as we entered the neat kitchen. Mrs Culshaw had been very busy baking bread as well as scones, and her handiwork was cooling on grilles on the kitchen dresser.

'I'd been wondering how I could get the food to George,' Mrs Culshaw said. 'I was thinking I'd wait until our Edna calls later this afternoon and I'd ask her if she would call down at the signal box with it on her way home.' While saying this she was busy spreading butter onto the scones she had cut in half for us. After placing two halves on a plate for each of us, she poured some lemonade into two glasses.

'You're not local lads, are you?' she said knowingly, 'so where do you come from?'

'Halton,' I said, 'but we've been trainspotting at Birdswood. Mr Culshaw asked if we had bikes because he wanted us to come here to collect his baggin.'

'It's a good job you were there then,' said Mrs Culshaw with another warm smile. 'I wouldn't like to think of him starving to death for lack of food. Are you enjoying your scones?'

'They're very nice, Mrs Culshaw,' mumbled Alan with his mouth rather full.

Mrs Culshaw busied herself with placing her husband's sandwiches, apple and cakes into a carrier bag while Alan and I finished our scones and lemonade. The carrier bag was made of thick brown kraft, the top of which was folded over and reinforced with a strip of cardboard. Two small string loop handles were threaded through holes punched in the top rim. Most grocery shops gave such bags to their customers to carry home their purchases, and if they survived the journey without tearing or getting soaked with rainwater, they were put by for other uses later on.

While doing this, she said, 'You haven't told me your names yet, have you? I ought to know who's doing this important errand for my poor, starving husband.'

We both told her who we were, by which time she had finished packing the food and we had stowed away our unexpected refreshments. Handing the bag to Alan, who had told her he had a saddlebag on his bike, Mrs Culshaw said, 'Now be careful on the main road on the way back, especially at workhouse corner.'

'We'll be careful, Mrs Culshaw,' I said, 'and thank you very much for the nice scones and lemonade.'

Alan added his thanks as Mrs Culshaw came as far as the front gate to see us on our way. On the journey back to the signal box we both agreed how nice she was and that her baking was first class. My own thoughts ranged over the cottage, its neat garden and lovely kitchen, the delicious smell of baking and the friendliness of the kind lady we had just met for the first time. It wasn't long, however, before we were talking about getting back into that signal box with all its excitement, and that seemed to make the return journey pass very quickly.

Instead of leaving our bikes in the usual place when we arrived back at Birdswood, we took them through the stock-proof gate, walked them up the steep path to the narrow meadow, then rode them along the grass to the point where we usually perched on the fence. As Alan unbuckled his saddlebag, I called out to Mr Culshaw who quickly appeared at the window to direct us over the lines and up to the signal box. He seemed very pleased we had accomplished our mission successfully and thanked us profusely for 'saving my life', as he put it. He said he was about to make a pot of tea and asked if we would like one, so, having generated a thirst from the cycle journey, we gladly accepted.

Surprisingly we didn't have to ask him if we could stay a while in the box. He offered by saying, 'Now then, here's the list of engines you missed while you were away fetching my food.' He handed me the list, then continued, 'I think if you stayed up here you'd have no trouble seeing the engines on the down Liverpool line, would you? Now what do you think of that idea?'

Our affirmative replies carried a great measure of excitement, which was suitably toned down when he went on to say, 'All right then, you can stay, but there are a few things you must remember if you want to visit me here, so that I don't get myself into trouble. So are you both listening carefully?'

After assuring him we were – we would have agreed to anything just to have the pleasure of staying in that elevated position where we could clearly see all the trains and know what was going on behind the scenes as well – he told us that we must not touch anything at all without his permission, we must be absolutely silent when he was using the telephone, and we must come away from the window whenever he said so. The significance and sensibleness of these restrictions would become clearer to us as time went on, but right then they did not seem to be onerous. And on reflection, wasn't Mr Culshaw implying that we could come again to the signal box in the future?

These arrangements having been made, Mr Culshaw set about making tea while Alan and

A dirty unidentifiable 'Black Five' hauls a Liverpool express past the signal box up the 1 in 151 gradient of the down Liverpool line in September 1960. The locomotive seems to be making very easy work of this difficult climb, steaming so freely that not only are the safety valves lifting but the fireman can well afford to take a breather at the cab window. This view highlights the difference in gradients of the down and up lines, the latter falling away from the camera past the signal box at 1 in 415. *R. Stephens*

The climb of the down Liverpool line at Birdswood is apparent again in this shot of Stanier 'Black Five' No 44869 piling on the power in order to lift this train to the top of the incline at Sutton Weaver on a September Saturday in 1960. Bordering the track here are the trees of Birds Wood, after which the nearby signal box – 200 yards out of shot to the right – was named. This view is looking towards Weaver Junction, just over a mile beyond the end of the train. The tracks in the foreground are the up and down West Coast Main Line, both of which have apparently been relaid with flat-bottom heavier-duty rail in preparation for the pending electrification from Weaver Junction northwards to Scotland and Liverpool, and sadly resulting in the demise of Birdswood signal box. *R. Stephens*

I checked the list of trains we'd missed. I personally was very disappointed to learn that the 'Princess Royal' engine we saw just as we set out on our ride to Preston-on-the-Hill was our old friend No 46203 *Princess Margaret Rose*. None of the other engines on the list were 'cops' for either of us, so it seemed that not only had we not missed anything special in the way of locomotives, but we had also begun a relationship with Mr and Mrs Culshaw that would give us immense pleasure for a long time to come.

Alan did get to pull a short-handled yellow signal lever as I had done earlier, and we learned that they were easy because they did not have any signal cable attached to them. They were just switches really, operating contacts that activated the mechanism of the down Distant signals at Weaver Junction, or, in the case of the lever I pulled earlier, operating the up colour-light Distant signal near Sutton Weaver. So the reason why the top part of the lever handle had been cut off was to indicate to the signalman that no great force was required to move it.

We were both mesmerised with all the activity that went on in this signal box located in such an important position as Birdswood, where two principal lines of the railway system diverged. For the most part we were content just to absorb the fantastic views of the traffic on the lines as seen from our new-found vantage point. I soon became firmly convinced that no locospotter could wish for any better place than this to watch the trains go by.

During the rest of that eventful afternoon Alan and I were spellbound, especially now that we could see the down Liverpool trains as well. But in truth that very same afternoon was the time when – I believe – my own interest in railways changed from merely seeing engines and noting their numbers to being intensely interested in how the railway worked. Matters were so absorbing that it was well after 5 o'clock before I realised the time, and we had to cycle back the 3 miles to Halton. We were certainly going to be late for tea that day, but what an excuse we'd have! I couldn't wait to get home to tell Mum and Dad what I'd been doing.

Bidding farewell to Mr Culshaw as we left the signal box, I could hardly believe my own ears when I heard him say, 'Next Saturday I'll be on early turn. If you want to come up here again you'll have to get here during the morning. I'd be pleased to see you.'

What an invitation! I was already planning how early I would get up next Saturday to make the most of that wonderful privilege.

8
BACK IN THE BOX

Long before going to bed that eventful day, all possible options for the following Saturday morning had been well and truly turned over in my mind so that, by the time I was ready to sleep, a positive plan had been established. Well, it seemed to me at the time that all options had been considered, but unfortunately one had completely escaped my notice. So that your reading enjoyment is not spoiled at this stage, I shall let it enter the story in its proper chronological position. I should also point out that the plans I had formulated had not yet been discussed with Alan Looker, but my contention was that if he was as thrilled about the prospect as I was, then he would agree to what I would put to him. You see, it would be Monday before the two of us would next meet and I couldn't possibly put the matter out of my mind until then, so naturally the plans I had drawn up were – to me at least – the only way to make the most of the fantastic offer Mr Culshaw had made just as we left him.

My plan was this: as Dad went to work a bit later on Saturday, I would ask him to give me a call to make sure I was up by 7 o'clock just before he left home, then after breakfast and all the other usual morning rituals I would cycle up the road to Alan's at 8 o'clock, from where we would cycle to Birdswood. The timetable sketched out in my mind would see us entering the signal box around 20 minutes to 9, giving us a few hours before Mr Culshaw finished his shift, assuming as I did that he would permit us to stay in the box that long. A

simple enough programme, I thought, for something as important as it was to me, so, having firmly established it in my mind, I drifted off into a deep, contented sleep. Strange as it may seem, I cannot remember dreaming about the exciting events of that day. The only explanation I can give for that is the anticipation of even more exciting things to come the following Saturday. Whether or not that was the reason I cannot say, but as matters turned out it could well have been right.

On the way to school on Monday morning neither Alan nor I mentioned our Saturday adventure, because we did not want to tell Barrie Dunbebin about our invitation in case he – as our close friend – felt he should be included. I could well anticipate the disappointment I should feel if three of us turned up at the signal box instead of the expected two, and the signalman refused to let us in. On the other hand, we would not want to withhold our secret from Barrie for too long, because surely that is what friends are for, to share good experiences together. Anyway, Barrie had begun to get very interested in photography, especially the developing and printing of film, and this new-found hobby had already begun to separate him from us on some of our trips to the railways of the area. Inevitably Barrie would learn of our visit to the signal box, but without conferring on the matter Alan and I had decided that now was not the time. So the discussions on our walk to school that morning centred on the First Division football results – an innocent enough subject, since each of us supported a different First Division team, and was sufficiently diverse from railways to avoid either Alan or myself 'letting the cat out of the bag'.

At this important time of the academic year it was expected that student concentration would be reaching its zenith, but regrettably mine was headed well and truly in the opposite direction. I just could not get out of my mind the bells, levers and other interesting things I had seen in that signal box, and I kept seeing the polished floor and sensing the atmosphere I had absorbed on last Saturday's visit there. I'm sorry to admit that some of the details of the wheatlands of New South Wales and the Reformation were lost on me, as anticipation built up for next Saturday's adventure. I could not wait for dinner time (as we called lunch time) so that Alan and I could discuss the plans I had made. After our second helping of jam roly-poly had been tucked away appreciatively, we went into the playground for a quiet discussion of the plans. To my complete amazement, Alan fully agreed with all the details and was just as excited at the prospect as I was.

Just then Barrie called out to us from the playground gate as he walked through onto the common where we played football. 'Come on, you two, we've got to get some practice in ready for St Edwards on Saturday.'

Had I been a rubber balloon, that would have been the moment someone stuck a pin in me. Instant deflation by four simple words: 'St Edwards on Saturday'. The enormity of my blunder struck me like a full rugby scrum and left me breathless and disoriented just as if I had been trampled on by a whole team. Why had that detail slipped my mind? That was the option I had not considered.

Looking at Alan, I said, 'I'd forgotten that. Now what do we do?'

Coming from a small village school where the pupils numbered only about a hundred between five and 15 years old (the school-leaving age had only recently been raised from 14) meant that we only just had enough boys between 11 and 15 to form a football team. As we played in the Runcorn Schools League

there were fixtures throughout the football season, one of which – away against St Edward's Roman Catholic School from Runcorn next Saturday – I had completely overlooked. It was simply out of the question to even begin thinking of not playing, because Alan was a good half-back and I was goalkeeper and there were no other boys who could take our places except some under 11 who were below the age threshold for the league. Our not playing would mean we couldn't form a team and our opponents could therefore claim the points. What a dilemma!

Alan had turned quite pale, looking really worried as he said, 'We've had it, Peter. We can't go. We can't let the team down.' As he turned towards me I could see that he was more than a little upset as he continued, 'What a pity it wasn't an afternoon game, then we could do both things. But Birdswood will have to wait for another Saturday.'

'Did I hear you mention Birdswood?' asked Barrie, who, because of our delaying, had come over to hurry us to football practice.

It immediately seemed like the right time to tell him of the invitation, which we did. Happily he didn't seem to want to be invited along himself; when he had heard the details of our conflicting loyalties, he simply said, 'Well then, you'll have to leave that until another time, won't you?'

The relief I felt from having levelled with Barrie seemed to surge over the disappointment I felt over the forthcoming football fixture, so that I was then able to put my mind to other things instead of having my thoughts fixed permanently on Birdswood signal box. So the next few days at school passed off normally until yet another shock-wave was delivered to Alan and me on Thursday afternoon at the start of our PE lesson, the final session for the day, which was held in the school playground because we had no gym. Our teacher, Mr Dodd, was also our football team coach and manager. He always accompanied us to games, at home or away, and usually had some good tactics to pass on to us. Having assembled the three classes together for the PE lesson, he started by saying:

'This information is for the football team

only. We have had a message from St Edward's School asking for the football match on Saturday to be postponed because most of their pupils are going away on a special trip that day. They ask if we can play the match the following Wednesday afternoon instead. I have agreed, and so there will be no game next Saturday. Is that clear?'

Was it clear? It certainly was, and you can be very sure which two pupils answered, 'Yes, Sir!' most loudly. I could hardly believe what I had just heard, and as I looked across to Alan I could see his broad grin from one ear almost to the other.

'Did I say something funny, Looker?' snapped Mr Dodd when he saw Alan's grinning face. Not expecting a reply, he launched into his PE instructions for the whole class. What he would have thought had he seen my grinning face as well I do not know, but eventually, as the exercises progressed and Alan and I approached each other in two opposite-moving lines, he said as we passed, 'Brilliant news, eh?'

He was gone before I replied, but it was indeed brilliant news that our trip to Birdswood signal box could now go ahead precisely as planned. All that pre-planning could soon be put into operation, with rich rewards perhaps even beyond our wildest dreams being reaped by us both. Saturday could not come quickly enough for me.

On the way home from school that day, we included Barrie in our excited talk about the pending visit. He was quite pleased for us, it seemed, but had a trip to Chester with his parents arranged for that same day, so his mind was on obtaining his first developing tank and printing frames for his photography. That made Alan and me feel so much better about our invitation to the signal box, because never once did Barrie ask if he could come with us or say he wished that sort of thing would happen to him. Clearly we could look forward to our special privilege without having to feel guilty that Barrie was not included. It was around this time, I believe, that Barrie's interests began to move away from railways to music and photography, and although we remained good pals until he left school to join the RAF as a boy-entrant, he

never again came with us on a single outing to watch the trains go by.

On Friday afternoon, when school had finished for the week, Alan and I walked home by way of Halton Castle to give us more time to finalise the details of tomorrow's expedition. These days it is said that a week is a long time in politics, but believe me, this particular week at school seemed like a whole term. Now it had ended as far as school was concerned, full attention could be directed toward much more important matters, with the trip to Birdswood signal box tomorrow right at the top of the list. In preparation I had decided to give my old bicycle a good oiling and a clean, making sure that the tyres were pumped up sufficiently and the loose rear mudguard was fixed with a replacement nut and bolt just in case it was going to rain tomorrow.

'Come on, Peter, it's 7 o'clock and a lovely day for your trip.' Dad's voice and gentle shaking of my shoulder introduced me to a truly memorable Saturday. After a heartier than usual breakfast – Mum had included fried bread and mushrooms with the more usual bacon, egg, sausage and tomato because 'you'll need some extra energy for such an early ride' – I left home slightly earlier than planned, only to find Alan astride his bike at his front gate waiting for me. We set off in high spirits on such a beautifully sunny morning, which still carried with it a freshness belying the fact that it was early April, and our journey to Dutton and Birdswood was enjoyed the more because of what lay at the end of it.

Alan's watch showed 8.24 as we reached the fence near the signal box, at which moment the Carlisle-Crewe parcels, running very late, came bustling along behind a rather grimy 'Crab'. Parcels trains always seemed to me to be untidy, consisting as they did of an infinite variety of non-passenger bogies with a few vans mixed in among them, and this particular train was no exception, well matched to the grubby locomotive. We would wait until Mr Culshaw came to the window to watch the train pass, then hope to catch his eye. Would he be very surprised to see us there so early?

As expected, he came to the window to

Made up of a variety of bogies and long-wheelbase vans, parcels trains were never glamorous but earned the railways a good deal of money. The fairly clean loco, 'Britannia' Class No 70032 *Tennyson*, is not typical for this Class C train signalled by the bell code 1-3-1, all vehicles of which conform to coaching stock requirement. *Derek Cross*

watch the parcels train pass by, but what took us by surprise was the rather serious look on his face and his order 'Stay there!' shouted down to us just after the last bogie of the parcels train passed under the flyover. We had no opportunity to question this order, as Mr Culshaw immediately left the window to see to the bells and levers as the train passed out of his section. If this development was having the same effect on Alan as it was on me, he would be feeling a sickness in the pit of his stomach right now. How disappointing to be so firmly ordered to 'Stay there!' when we had actually been invited to visit the signal box. Surely Mr Culshaw couldn't have forgotten that he had invited us? He seemed such a genuine man last week when we had done the favour for him. It could not be possible that such a nice man would also be two-faced, saying one thing one minute and doing just the opposite the next. No, he didn't strike me as being that type of person, rather someone who could have fitted well into the mould of grandfather. Both my grandfathers died before I was born, so I never knew them, but when I met Mr Culshaw last week I formed the impression that he had qualities I would expect my grandfathers to have displayed: a warmth and kindness tempered with firmness without being rigid, very understanding and helpful with a tinge of humour. So what had gone wrong for us to be ordered to 'Stay there!'?

A few seconds later the answer to this dilemma was made very clear when Mr Culshaw reappeared at the signal box window with a smile on his face. Looking down in our direction, he shouted, 'Hang on there for another couple of minutes – there's a down excursion train just round the corner. As soon as it's passed, you can safely cross the line and come up.'

'Thanks, Mr Culshaw,' I replied. What a sense of relief I felt on hearing that. In all the excitement of anticipating this visit to the signal box, I hadn't noticed that the Down Main Starter was off, otherwise it would have been obvious to me that we could not safely cross the line. Looking at Alan it was quite clear that he, too, was relieved that nothing had gone wrong, because he was wearing his wide grin again. Once more Mr Culshaw disappeared from the window just as the sound of an express passenger train could be heard approaching the Down Home signal. We climbed up onto the wooden fence to watch it pass, hauled by a rather odd-looking 'Black Five', No 44687. Although my mind was focussed on climbing the signal box steps in just a few minutes time, the engine passing in front of us did look as though it had been in a front-end collision and had been hastily repaired. It was only some considerable time later that I learned that the locomotive had been fitted with Caprotti valve gear. On any other occasion the unusual features of the

'Mickey', as we called the Stanier 5MT engines, would have fuelled debate for half an hour or so, but today there is something much more important claiming our attention. Immediately the last coach passed we jumped down off the fence, crossed the line after looking both ways and made our way excitedly up the path to the signal box steps. Climbing them for this second time was just as exciting as the first, perhaps even more so because I knew we would be spending a few hours inside the box.

It is hard to put into words the intense feeling of excitement I enjoyed as – for the second Saturday in succession – I climbed those sturdy wooden steps up to the signal box. Even though it was only seven days previously that we had been in this situation, it was almost as if that occasion had never happened and today was the first time such a marvellous privilege was being extended to us. Oh, yes! The vivid memory of that shiny expanse of polished floor was still in my mind, being confirmed as a reality a few seconds later, but what about all the other interesting things I'd never seen before until last week? They could all be rediscovered again today without Alan and I having to break off in order to fetch Mr Culshaw's food, so we could give all the items of equipment our fullest and undivided attention, find out all about their function and – who knows – even be allowed to operate some of them.

Just at this point in the process of recalling memories from almost 50 years ago, one thing hits home most poignantly. Why, oh why, did I not make any notes of all the technical information Mr Culshaw passed on to me about the signal box and its apparatus, exactly how it worked and what one was expected to do with it? Why did I not think to borrow Dad's camera and Barrie's flash unit to take one or two photographs of the inside of this fascinating workplace? Even though Birdswood was located off the beaten track, there have been many photographs taken of it from the outside, but so far in my researches I have not been able to track down a single interior picture.

Just as we entered the signal box again a bell rang and Mr Culshaw, who had been welcoming us into the box, glanced towards some instruments above the signal levers, then at the clock, and went to write something briefly in a book on a desk just inside the door.

'That was the excursion train that just went down,' he said, turning away from his desk and looking in our direction. We were standing just about in the middle of the floor. 'It has just gone out of section at Norton Crossing,' he went on, 'but I'll explain all about that eventually. Sit yourselves down on those lockers while I make us all a nice cup of tea.'

Almost immediately the same bell rang out four short beats, which diverted Mr Culshaw's attention away from tea-making to the instruments above the signal levers. He pressed a button on the front of one of the instruments and turned a black knob, then went to the next instrument and pressed the button on that in the same way. Just as he turned towards us as if to say something, a different bell sounded out four clear rings. Right away Mr Culshaw took hold of one of the signal levers and pulled it back so that it stuck out into the room, then the next one was treated the same. Both these levers had red-painted stems, but the next one, painted yellow, seemed to need much more muscle-power to pull off than the others. Having dealt with the three levers, Mr Culshaw then went to the desk to write in his book, which I later learned was called the Train Register. As he did so, he said that soon the up express from Morecambe to Crewe would pass along the up main line and that if we wanted to see it we must view it through a gap beneath the cluster of telephones and the desk.

'It's running just about 11 minutes late at the moment, so I expect the driver will be doing his best to be on time at Crewe. By the way, the DSO from Warrington usually goes to Crewe on this train,' he said, 'and if he sees you watching him from the window I'll be in trouble.' He explained that the DSO was a sort of area manager, and he didn't want to get on the wrong side of him.

He told us that the red signal levers worked the Home and Starter signals, and pointed out where they were. I could see the arms raised up at 45 degrees, and also noticed that beneath each was a yellow arm with a fish-tailed end, and these too were raised up. Mr Culshaw said that these were Distant signals for Weaver Junction, the next section along. He told us that the yellow lever he had just pulled worked the Birdswood Distant signal, which was 1,470 yards away, well beyond Dutton Tunnel where the up and down main lines disappeared from view.

An old kettle was boiling as it sat on top of the shiny black free-standing iron stove roughly halfway along the wall opposite the signal levers, and Mr Culshaw poured the boiling water into a brown earthenware teapot.

'Not be long now,' he said with a smile as he stirred the tea with a dessert spoon. 'Do you both take sugar?' He noted our affirmative

reply by spooning in two large measures of sugar, which were vigorously stirred, then, handing one to each of us, he said, 'Remember when you were here last week I told you not to touch anything at all unless I say so?' We both nodded. 'And I said you must be silent when I'm on the phone. Well, that's so that I sha'n't get into trouble if anybody in authority thinks you're here. If I want you to do anything, I'll tell you what to do and how to do it, but first of all just drink your tea, have a look around and ask any questions you like. While I'm seeing to the trains, I'll explain how I'm working the box and try to answer any of your questions.'

Just then two rings on the first bell broke the silence, and Mr Culshaw went to an

'Royal Scot' Class 4-6-0 No 46161 *The King's Own* speeds an up express from Glasgow towards Birdswood on Saturday 25 July 1959. The rear two coaches are inside the 84-yard-long Dutton Tunnel, over which the A533 Runcorn to Northwich road runs from left to right. *J. A. Peden*

Another 'Royal Scot', No 46146 *The Rifle Brigade,* heads south with an express from Blackpool during the spring of 1960. Birdswood signal box stands prominently beside the up Liverpool line, and this photograph shows the excellent position chosen for it so that the signalman would have an uninterrupted view of all tracks under his control. But not for long now, because work is well in hand for the electrification north of Weaver Junction, which would in due course lead to the box's closure and demolition. *R. Stephens*

instrument and turned a black knob, which altered the position of a needle on the instrument. Going back to the desk to write down the time of that last bell code, Mr Culshaw said, 'It's just passing Norton Crossing now, so in 2 minutes you'll see it come through the tunnel. Don't forget, keep out of sight by the telephones. You should be able to get the number from there.'

Not long afterwards the train came into view as it left Dutton Tunnel, almost half a mile away, and was making good progress hauled by a Stanier 'Black Five'.

Mr Culshaw went to the instruments as the train got near and tapped out a code on the end instrument, then right away went to the window to watch the train pass. Loaded with only eight coaches and by now running on the level, the engine seemed to have the task very much in hand, and I recall logging the number 45306 in my notebook. As the last coach passed along the up line way below our vantage point, Mr Culshaw said, 'Tail lamp complete', then went back to the instruments, all the time watching until the rear of the train passed the Up Starting signal. He then released the levers, which caused the elevated signal arms to fall back to the horizontal position, and tapped out another code and turned the black knob on one of the instruments. Finally he returned to the book on the desk and again entered some times relative to the train. As I was watching all this, it seemed to me that in the course of a shift, a signalman may walk miles to and fro across the floor of the signal box while attending to his duties.

Perhaps anticipating a short period of quietness before the next train was due, Mr Culshaw sat on his seat next to the booking desk, picked up the *Daily Express* of the day before and began to read. It hadn't occurred to me at the time but, thinking back, how appropriate that a railwayman should read that newspaper, rather like a postman opting for the *Daily Mail* or a watchmaker preferring *The Times*! Not wishing to intrude by asking questions, Alan and I were content to sit there and take a mental note of the many different fittings and items of equipment that made up this really interesting workplace.

At this point I will describe the layout of the signal box, especially as – at the time of writing – I have been unable to locate a photograph of its interior. It could be argued that the inside of one box is very much like another apart from size, but I will describe it here so that a mental picture can be formed.

On entering the box through the outward-opening door in the gable end, the eye was drawn immediately to the 20 levers coloured red, yellow, black, and black and white, grouped in one bank of 15 and one bank of five, set centrally along the length of the floor. Between the two banks was a gap wide enough to pass through, but anyone doing so would have to duck to avoid striking his head against the block shelf, which was suspended about 5 feet above floor level. The levers, with their highly polished bare-metal handles, looked attractive and clean. On the floor in front of them was a long piece of bare timber, thicker at the side nearest the levers, and I noticed that Mr Culshaw placed his foot on this wedge-shaped board when pulling off the levers. Behind the frame was a narrow black-painted board mounted almost vertically about a foot above floor level. Screwed on it and aligned with each lever was a small cast iron plate painted the same colour as the lever in front of it, identifying its function. The black levers had two such plates per lever.

The block shelf itself was truly fascinating, carrying as it did all the many different instruments needed to maintain the 'absolute block system' of signalling. There were four twin-needle telegraphs, each in a varnished timber case, and each case was mounted upon four short bronze pillars between which was a large bell. Several other varnished timber boxes containing electrical locking apparatus were also mounted on the shelf, but these had no dials or indicators. Affixed along the front face of the shelf were several small instruments, some circular with glass fronts containing what looked for all the world like miniature signal arms; others were rectangular Bakelite cases housing small coloured lights. Looking completely out of place among this fine array were two black metal elongated hoops about 7 inches long by 3 inches wide, the use of which will be mentioned later. The

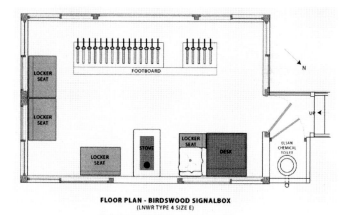

FLOOR PLAN - BIRDSWOOD SIGNALBOX
(LNWR TYPE 4 SIZE E)

Above I have not yet come across any photographs taken inside Birdswood signal box, and so will use this one of the similar but slightly larger Weaver Junction box. There are, however, some fundamental differences shown in this 1959 photograph. The track diagram has been prepared for when Birdswood box would be demolished a year or two later; it is not shown in its position inside the 'V' at the left of the diagram. Note the gradient profiles for each track drawn in the margins. The Birdswood diagram was not illuminated with lamps indicating the presence of a train on the line. On the block shelf are typical LNWR block instruments (Birdswood had four) together with indicators and repeaters that show the status of signals out of sight. Unlike Birdswood, here the telephones are fitted to the block shelf, which at a junction as busy as this is sensible, even if they do make the shelf look a bit untidy. Another difference relates to the Webb-pattern levers, the handles of which are painted white whereas at Birdswood they were polished. It is surprising that in total this box had only four levers more than Birdswood,

despite being a junction and having a goods loop off the up Liverpool line. *Norman Jones*

Above Birdswood was an LNWR Type 4 size E brick-to-floor structure measuring 18ft 9in long by 12 feet wide, oriented facing south-west onto the branch lines. The operating floor was about 8 feet above rail level. *S. Haddock*

shelf was suspended from the underside of the ceiling by stout metal rods painted black. Also hanging from the ceiling above the instruments on the block shelf was a large diagram, which showed the layout of the tracks controlled by the signals operated from this box, and suspended precisely above the centre of the floor was a pressure-type Tilley lamp.

Hanging on the wall over the door was a red flag and a green flag, each rolled around its wooden handle, a brass hunting horn and an old-fashioned megaphone. On the left immediately inside the door was a narrow cupboard about wardrobe height, then a typical LNWR desk up against the back wall. Above the desk four telephones were mounted on a piece of wood fixed across a window frame, over the top of which was the traditional railway clock. Next to the desk was a wooden locker, fitted out with some old upholstery cushions to form a makeshift easy chair, which was separated from the cast-iron stove by a narrow space, just wide enough to permit entry for the signalman's legs. The stove stood on a cast-iron hearth, which for safety reasons hade an upstand all around to contain any straying hot embers. Rising vertically from the flat top of the stove and exiting through the roof was a cast-iron stove pipe. This ensemble was made complete by the black cast-iron kettle that was almost continually on the boil. Beyond the stove was another low locker, then a small space in the corner, which allowed the signalman room to go to the window to observe trains on the main lines. Facing the door and against the wall at the far end of the box were two more low lockers.

Although it takes time to describe the inside of the box, all the details were taken in during a very brief period, at the end of which one of the bells rang out a code of 2-1. I was quite startled by this, yet to my surprise Mr Culshaw moved not a muscle. I looked at him for quite a few seconds before I realised that he was peering over the top of his reading glasses at me. Then, putting aside his newspaper, he said, 'It's all right, Pete – that was just Weaver Junction letting me know that last train has left his section on its way south. Apart from

noting the time in the Train Register, I need do nothing. So that's us finished with that one!'

He then got up from his seat and, turning to the desk, said, 'If you'd both like to come over here, I'll explain the Train Register to you. You'll probably forget most of it, but never mind, I can take you through it again some time in the future.'

With that he entered the time of 8.43 in what seemed to be the last column on the right to be used, then went on to explain the purpose of the Train Register and what had to be entered in the various columns. I found it fascinating that someone could compare entries in registers from adjacent signal boxes and, with experience, tell if entries were being properly made. I learned that entries were to be made at the time of the event, not some later time when the actual times may have been forgotten. Accuracy to half a minute was vitally important.

With so much to see and plenty of information to take in, it seemed almost sacrilegious to be even thinking of noting engine numbers, but at this stage that is just what Alan and I continued to do. What a magnificent platform from which to view passing trains, spoiled at this stage only by the fact that we both had to keep out of sight of any railway employees who may have been travelling on the passing trains. However, it was not long before Mr Culshaw had thought up an ingenious way around this irritating problem. We had been there not much more than an hour when he broke off from explaining about adjusting the tension in the wire of the Up Main Distant signal and said, 'Hey, I've just had a brainwave that you might like.'

He walked over to the cupboard just inside the door and took out a railway-issue waistcoat. Holding it out towards us he explained, 'One of you could wear this if you want to watch from the window, then anyone looking out from the train will think you're the signalman or a box lad.' I was stunned by the absolute simplicity of this solution, and must have stood there with my mouth open as Alan, who was nearer to Mr Culshaw than I, stepped forward and took the waistcoat. We were both wearing long dark school trousers, having just graduated from short ones, so the appearance to travellers would be that of a railway uniform, especially as we had on white long-sleeved shirts.

It was not long before Alan was dressed to stand at the window, and at Mr Culshaw's wise suggestion we agreed to change over about every half hour. As if to make up for not wearing the waistcoat, Mr Culshaw allowed me to release the signal levers under his direction after a train has passed. Of course it required no effort, because the balance weights at the signal post did the work, but care was needed to prevent the levers slamming back into the frame. When it came to my turn for the uniform, I really felt the part and began to enjoy watching the passing trains from the open windows of this vantage point. It was only in the case of up trains on the Liverpool branch that I could not lean out of the window, because the up track passed immediately in front of the box, so to get the number of the locomotive I found it best to stand at the door and watch it approach from there.

I have in my collection of railway artefacts a waistcoat of precisely the same style as the one I wore in the box. Despite being of British Railways issue, it carries five chromium-plated LMS buttons and is officially known as a vest. The front panels are of black serge and it has long sleeves with a split cuff, the sleeves and the back being of heavy black linen. The garment is lined throughout with a cream cotton material, with two pockets on the left breast and one on the right. Sadly it is several sizes too small for me to wear, but just looking at it brings back fond memories.

Going back now to that memorable Saturday in 1951, Alan and I had some truly wonderful experiences, together with several cups of the renowned signal box tea, and we enjoyed our sandwich lunch taken while sitting on one of the wooden lockers that

served as seats for any railwaymen who visited. Happily Alan and I were the only visitors that day so there was no need for us to suddenly vacate the box before we were seen, but we did have to leave at a quarter to two because Ernie Antrobus, Mr Culshaw's relief, was in the habit of arriving about 5 minutes early. He would approach the box from the direction of the up main bracket signal, so our paths should not cross. So that we wouldn't be seen leaving the box, we went down to where our bikes were leaning against the fence. If by any chance Mr Antrobus saw us there, he would think we were just the usual trainspotters. However, because merely watching the trains from the lineside would have been such an anti-climax after our long stay in the signal box, we decided to savour the experience and cycle home right away.

During that morning shift from 6.00am to 2.00pm Mr Culshaw would have been involved in dealing with around 90 trains of almost every type, averaging one train every 5.3 minutes. All the details of these movements, together with the other two shifts covering the full 24 hours, can be seen in Appendix 1. The afternoon shift had about the same number of train movements, but the night shift was very much busier, showing an average of one train every 3.5 minutes. Quite a busy box for a block post!

So instead of spending our Saturday morning playing football for the school team, we had something very much more exciting to reflect upon, many additional memories to store up, and further visits to make to the signal box in the future. Although we had not made any positive arrangements with Mr Culshaw for visiting again, we knew his shift pattern and would wait for his invitation to cross the line and climb the steps when he was next working the afternoon shift. Then once again our vivid railway dreams could become reality.

9
LOCAL RAILWAYS

This quite small area of railways contains some very interesting features: two noteworthy viaducts, two tunnels (although one is so short that as a boy I used to refer to it as a bridge), a level crossing, water troughs, an aqueduct, a flyover and a flying junction. True, there are no main-line stations, locomotive works or grandiose railway buildings, but nevertheless it is an area brimming with fascination, with a goodly length of the old LNWR 'Premier Line' into the bargain. The majority of readers will not be familiar with the terrain in this part of the railway system, though they may well have heard of some of the locations, such as Weaver Junction or Acton Grange Junction. So in

order that the reader may better understand the narrative, I shall now describe, section by section, the railways with which this book is concerned.

WEAVER JUNCTION TO ACTON GRANGE JUNCTION

Weaver Junction was situated to the north of a lovely sandstone viaduct carrying the West Coast Main Line over the beautiful valley of the River Weaver. The signal box here was very isolated amid the north Cheshire countryside, with the consequence that only the most determined railway photographers ever found their way to it. At this location a

It can be seen from this 1960 photograph that Weaver Junction signal box was taller than Birdswood. Apart from its height above track level, this LNWR brick-to-floor Type 4 signal box was the same size as Birdswood, known as size E, established by noting the window configuration along the front: two panels sliding, three centre panels fixed, then two more sliding panels. The total length was 18 ft 9 in and the width 12 feet. A size E cabin could accommodate up to 25 levers; Weaver Junction had 24 but Birdswood had only 20. *Norman Jones*

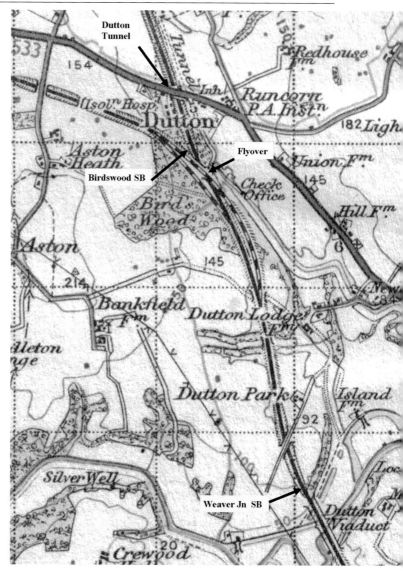

Weaver Junction and Birdswood.
Crown Copyright; reproduced from the 1947 1-inch map, Sheet 100, with the kind permission of Ordnance Survey

so-called 'flying junction' presented long-bladed facing points to down trains from Acton Bridge (not to be confused with Acton Grange Junction further north), which would attain a good turn of speed; a permanent speed restriction of 50mph was therefore placed upon it. From the junction the down main track, ie the West Coast Main Line, and the down branch to Liverpool ran side by side as far as Birdswood.

Weaver Junction signal box was on the west side of the line at the junction, and the operating floor was about 15 feet above track level, with a straight run of 22 wooden steps leading up to the door at the south end. A typical LNWR Type 4 box, it was size E, housing some 25 levers. Although I went inside this box once, I cannot recall it being much different from Birdswood, except for housing a few more levers. That in no way over-simplifies the work of this box, however, because it not only had the points on the main lines to deal with, but also the signalman had to 'regulate' traffic running southwards.

It seems rather a shame that Weaver Junction box was demolished during the electrification north of that point in the early 1960s. The replacement electronic panel was sited on the east side of the tracks about 400 yards north of the viaduct, nearer to Birdswood, where the signal box had also been demolished by that time as part of the upgrading of the West Coast Main Line. Sadly, though, Birdswood box was not replaced.

As the tracks proceed northwards from Weaver Junction, the terrain changes from a river valley into gently undulating agricultural land through which the Grand Junction Railway had been cut by Joseph Locke in the mid-1830s. It is sobering to think that this line was surveyed, built and opened only a few years after the Rainhill Trials when Stephenson's *Rocket* and suchlike locomotives were in their infancy. Since the land to the west of the track hereabouts rises towards the village of Aston, while that on the east side drops slightly away in the direction of Dutton Park Farm and the Trent & Mersey Canal, the effect is one of being in a cutting if one looks west, and on an embankment if one looks east. However, such terrain prevails only for half a mile or so, because the up Liverpool line, running towards us down its embankment, is met on the east side of the track.

Entering the Birdswood section, the West

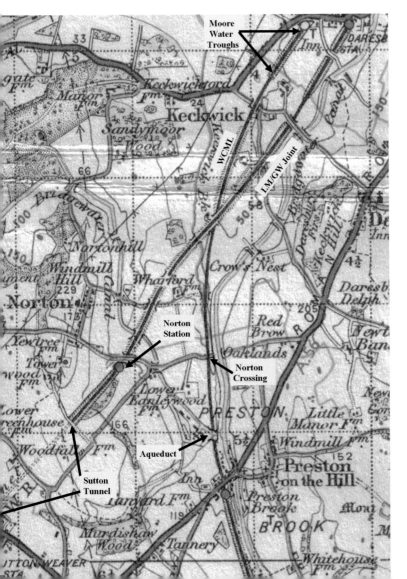

Preston Brook to Moore. *Crown Copyright; reproduced from the 1947 1-inch map, Sheet 100, with the kind permission of Ordnance Survey*

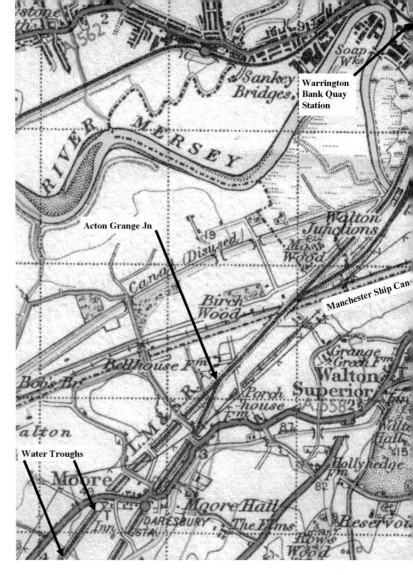

Coast Main Line continues northwards on the level, but the down Liverpool branch, which up to now has run parallel to it, begins climbing and curving away to the west. More of that later. Meanwhile the main line passes beneath the flyover, next to which Birdswood signal box stood prominently on the embankment to the left, unique in that it was a block post for two separate main lines. Continuing northwards on the level, the line now curves almost imperceptibly to the right. At milepost 176, just over a quarter of a mile north of Birdswood box, the level section gives way to a 1 in 180 falling gradient through the 84-yard-long Dutton Tunnel and on to Preston Brook. There the signal box stood alongside the down line about 500 yards

before the small disused station and an overbridge carrying the A56 road through the village. On the up side opposite the signal box was the access to a goods yard, where a small goods shed and three short roads once accommodated the needs of the tradespeople of the local community. A 'cripple' siding about a hundred yards long ran alongside the up track.

Continuing down about 400 yards beyond the road overbridge, we find an interesting feature in the form of an aqueduct, which carries the Bridgewater Canal over the railway near the point where it joins the Trent & Mersey Canal. A further half-mile northwards brings us to Norton Crossing, where the signal box, with its 10-lever frame, stood beside the down line right next to the gated road-crossing. Still on a falling gradient and now virtually level with the surrounding fields, we continue a further mile before we pass beneath the LMR/WR jointly operated Warrington-Chester line. The track then runs onto the perfectly level section where Moore water troughs stood. Once through the disused station at Moore, the line climbs steeply at 1 in 135 to Acton Grange Junction, where the Chester to Warrington line filters in from our right. The climb continues for a few hundred yards more to cross the Manchester Ship Canal by means of a fairly distinctive multi-lattice girder bridge, immediately beyond which was an extensive layout of sidings near to Walton Old Junction. Thereafter it is downhill for almost 2 miles to Warrington Bank Quay station, then on to Wigan, Preston, Lancaster, Carlisle and Scotland.

ACTON GRANGE JUNCTION TO FRODSHAM JUNCTION

If we now start from Acton Grange Junction on the West Coast Main Line and proceed generally southwards, taking the branch line heading for Chester, we come onto a section of line that was operated jointly by the London Midland and Western Regions of British Railways. After a short section on a falling gradient we begin a variable climb that reaches a summit in the middle of Sutton Tunnel, but more of that later. A mile from Acton Grange Junction finds this branch line riding along the top of an embankment, crossing the West Coast Main Line by means of a graceful double-arch bridge. A further mile and a half brings us to the site of the archetypal country station of Norton. Here the influence of the former Great Western Railway was detected in the architecture, the angled running-in boards and the LMS/GWR Joint-type signal box. The photograph on page 20 shows this lovely little station, which was flanked by a road overbridge carrying a country lane from the hamlet of Norton down to Norton Crossing.

Beyond the station the line follows a gentle curve to the right and after about a quarter of a mile enters Sutton Tunnel, 1 mile 154 yards long, with three ventilation shafts, which fascinated me as a boy. The tunnel portals are in fine sandstone, well-weathered, giving the structure a classic appearance. Roughly midway through the tunnel the summit of the climb is reached, after which the downhill run at 1 in 264 goes all the way to the viaduct just beyond Frodsham Junction. Half a mile before reaching there, however, was Halton station, almost a mirror image of Norton. Just beyond the western end of the platforms a goods loop turned off to the left and wound its way behind the LNWR-type signal box to continue parallel to the running lines as far as Frodsham Junction, just over a quarter of a mile beyond the station, where the branch joins the Chester to Liverpool line.

Looking north along the West Coast Main Line towards Warrington, Stanier 'Pacific' No 46228 *Duchess of Rutland* hauls an up Scottish express past Acton Grange Junction on Friday 15 May 1959. The line to Chester runs away to the right above the caravans. On the horizon behind the train is the unmistakable outline of the bridges over the Manchester Ship Canal. Walton Old Junction, with a fairly extensive goods yard, lies beyond, with Warrington Bank Quay station 2 miles further down the line. *J. A. Peden*

Frodsham Junction and Halton Junction. *Crown Copyright; reproduced from the 1947 1-inch map, Sheet 100, with the kind permission of Ordnance Survey*

FRODSHAM JUNCTION TO HALTON JUNCTION

Turning back here, we now take the line from Frodsham Junction that swung away to the north-west. This was part of the Chester-Liverpool route, and climbed quite steeply, first on a high embankment, then into a cutting, for the short section of about 1¾ miles to Halton Junction, where it joined the Crewe-Liverpool line right at the LNWR signal box that supervised this junction.

HALTON JUNCTION TO WEAVER JUNCTION

This section of the up Liverpool branch line is almost 5 miles in length and takes us past

Birdswood and back to the point where we started. Climbing at 1 in 115 as it passed Halton Junction in a cutting, the line was accompanied by a down loop on the right immediately after the signal box. The line runs south-easterly and is crossed by two unmade farm tracks, curving gently more towards the east as it breasts a summit just after becoming level with the surrounding land. However, the fields alongside begin to fall away as the railway takes to an embankment, running downhill at 1 in 323 for almost half a mile.

Just west of Yellow Bridge the goods loop diverged from the down line, while the up line – still on the embankment – began a gentle climb at 1 in 549 to pass Sutton Weaver signal box on the left after almost half a mile. The

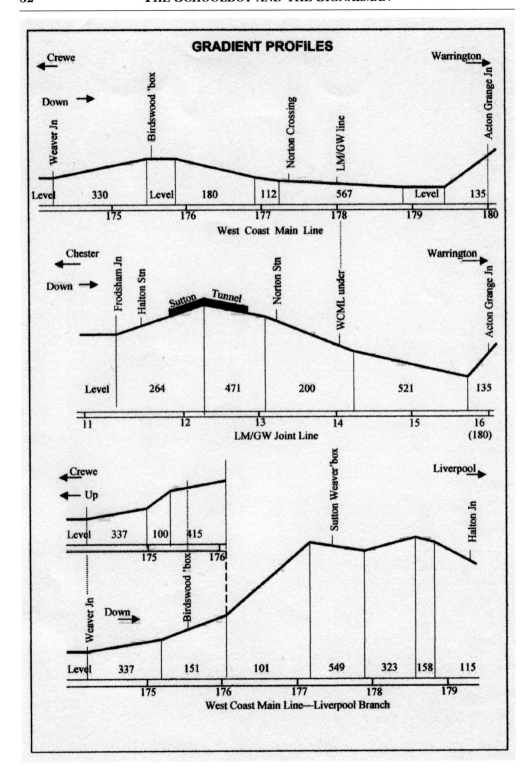

GRADIENT PROFILES

A down Liverpool express hauled by grubby Stanier Class 5 No 45419 passes the signal box at Sutton Weaver after climbing the steep gradient from Birdswood in 1960; work on electrification is being carried out. Almost directly beneath this signal box Sutton Tunnel accommodated the Warrington-Chester line operated jointly by the London Midland and Western Regions. *R. Stephens*

Stanier 'Black Five' No 45005 hauls a down local Crewe-Liverpool train up the stiff 1 in 151 incline towards Sutton Weaver in September 1960, showing the difference in levels between the up and down Liverpool tracks. For this train the rate of climb increases from here to 1 in 101 for about another mile. Birdswood signal box lies about a quarter of a mile behind the train around the corner. *R. Stephens*

climb continues for a further 25 chains until just after the A56 road is crossed, at which point a dramatic change occurs, the line now running steeply downhill at 1 in 101 for a few chains more than a mile. Just over half a mile further on was Birdswood signal box; remember that the line we are now traversing – the up Liverpool – crosses over the West Coast Main Line at the Birdswood flyover, while the down Liverpool track lies at approximately the same level as the West Coast Main Line at the flyover. Quite obviously, then, the gradient profiles for the up and down line will be different, and it is from this point that the variation occurs. While the down Liverpool track climbs

towards us at 1 in 151, the up line falls at a much more moderate gradient of 1 in 415, past the site of Birdswood signal box and across the flyover. Directly thereafter the rate of fall increases to 1 in 100 for about a quarter of a mile until it attains the same level as the West Coast Main Line. At this point a loop diverged to our left and followed the same course as the up track until just before Weaver Junction; thus at this point there were five running lines side by side on the gradient of 1 in 337: up Liverpool loop, up Liverpool, up main, down main and down Liverpool. Just a few more chains southwards is Weaver Junction, where the signal box was located on our right.

Rebuilt 'Royal Scot' Class 4-6-0 No 46119 *Lancashire Fusilier* coasts down the incline of the up Liverpool track past Birdswood's Home signal with an express bound for the West of England. Birdswood signal box is about 6 chains ahead of the locomotive, and the down Liverpool track can be seen on the left climbing steeply towards Sutton Weaver. *R. Stephens*

By the way, as remodelling work was carried out prior to electrification, the up loop and up Liverpool tracks were transposed, so that the loop lay between the up main and up Liverpool tracks. Also, the flying junction for down traffic at this location was moved northwards about a mile so that the Liverpool branch peeled off just a few chains before the flyover at Birdswood.

Apart from the obvious difference in gradients of the up and down Liverpool branch lines, there are a few additional features associated with the down track that ought to be mentioned. For instance, because the down track as it leaves the main lines just before Birdswood curves fairly sharply towards the west, and is bounded by the trees of Bird's Wood (after which this section of railway was named), the Down Home signal to the left of the track became more and more difficult to see from a distance as the trees matured and grew. Therefore to improve visibility and to give drivers an earlier sighting of its aspect, a much taller post of the lattice type was positioned to the right of the running line and worked in conjunction with the original, operated by lever 17 at Birdswood. About 5 chains beyond the Home signal (there was no separate Starting signal on this down track) a set of spring-loaded catch points was positioned to protect any train standing at the Home signal from the possibility of collision from runaway vehicles that may have broken away from a preceding train. If at any time wrong-line working was instituted on the down Liverpool track, lever number 8 could be pulled off to close these points to permit such manoeuvres. Further down the track towards Sutton Weaver (ie going uphill) a rather more complex set of catch points was located close to the road overbridge carrying Aston Lane from the A533 to Aston Heath. Because the line was in a cutting here, a short length of track was joined to the catch points to carry any runaway vehicles up the embankment, their momentum propelling them off the end of this short track into the field at the side and out of harm's way. Two photographs of this arrangement can be seen on page 112.

10
FINDING THE SECOND TREASURE

This chapter is all about the time I was heaving coal from the tender of a light engine when Joan Hazlehurst came by taking her little corgi dog for a walk. Mr Culshaw introduced us when she came back along the public footpath that passed beside the signal box, and hey presto! That was it! I had fallen head over heels in love again – this time not with a signal box, but with a lovely girl whose feminine charms were to prove more attractive to me than all the delights the railway had to offer put together. But wait! The subject of this chapter has been divulged in just one short paragraph, so let us backtrack to flesh out more of the fine details, because in this episode there is a good deal of railway interest.

It was Saturday 18 April 1953 and a typically beautiful sunny afternoon. Mr Culshaw was on his last 2-to-10 shift of the week and I had cycled over from Halton to spend the afternoon working the box. I really enjoyed Saturdays like this, simply because I could spend the whole afternoon at Birdswood practising the art of railway signalling under the keen, watchful eye of the ever-vigilant Mr Culshaw. Lovely though the afternoon was, the condition of the weather was not really important so long as there was no fog. Fog meant that I would not be able to go up into the box because there would be local platelayers called out to act as fogmen, and you could never be sure who they might talk to in one of those unguarded moments about 'that young lad who visits George in the box'. However, on this particular day there was no such thing as fog, and all was going really well with – as usual – plenty of trains to keep me busy.

It was not more than about half an hour after my arrival that the teapot was brought out and a brew of tea made for the two of us to enjoy. I say 'the two of us' because it was very rare that the drink was shared with anyone else as, under normal working conditions, there would only be Mr Culshaw and myself in the box.

On an odd occasion we were joined by a fireman from an engine that was held up by an adverse signal; under Rule 55 it was necessary for a member of the train crew to go to the signal box to 'remind the signalman of the position of the train'. However, this was not necessary where a white diamond was displayed on the post of the signal, unless 'the train be detained an unusually long time'. For an anxious train crew heading back to their home shed, a stand of anything more than about 3 minutes would certainly be considered an unusually long time, so it would normally be the fireman who would carry out this procedure, even though the white diamond signified that the presence of his train was clearly indicated to the signalman by a track circuit instrument on the block shelf. So, in order to explain my presence in the box should it ever become necessary, Mr Culshaw would say that he had come to work without his baggin and that his wife had sent me to bring it to him. To me this sounded plausible enough, but I'm not so sure that anyone finding me in the signal box would be convinced! Anyway, I can't recall this excuse ever having to be used, as more often than not a fireman was just not interested in why a young lad should be there, especially if he was offered a cup of tea.

While drinking his tea Mr Culshaw was taking a careful look at the current Weekly Notices, and after a few minutes looked over to me and said, 'I'm going to have to stop a light engine on its way to Crewe Works later this afternoon, Pete, because we're getting short of coal and our delivery is not due until the end of next week.'

'Well, if it's light, it won't be pulling any coal wagons, will it,' was my immediate reply. But I might have known Mr Culshaw knew what he was doing.

Part of page 59 from the 1950 edition of the British Railways Rule Book (as amended) showing the Rule 55 diamond on a stop signal post; many of the photographs in this book show this white diamond. The sign in the lower diagram indicates that a call plunger is provided.

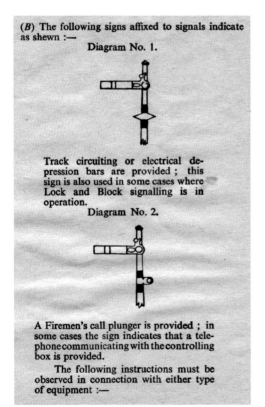

(B) The following signs affixed to signals indicate as shewn :—

Diagram No. 1.

Track circuiting or electrical depression bars are provided ; this sign is also used in some cases where Lock and Block signalling is in operation.

Diagram No. 2.

A Firemen's call plunger is provided ; in some cases the sign indicates that a telephone communicating with the controlling box is provided.

The following instructions must be observed in connection with either type of equipment :—

'You're right, Pete, but there could be quite a bit left in the tender, and if it's going to the Works it will not be needing much coal. I reckon I can persuade the footplate crew to let us have a bit just to keep us going.'

What a good idea, I thought to myself, because coming along the up line from Edge Hill shed it would pass right alongside the box, and as our now-empty coal bunker was right next to the running line, it would be easy to shovel coal from the engine into the bunker. Then something else occurred to me.

'Will you get into trouble for stopping the engine just for that?' I asked, but should have known better, because if that were so, Mr Culshaw would never have suggested it in the first place.

'Oh, no, Pete, it'll only be a couple of minutes, and there's nothing behind him until the Edge Hill-Bushbury due past us at 4.23, and if he's running to time he'd have to stand at Weaver Junction for a few minutes anyway until the up Perth has passed, so for him it won't make a bit of difference whether he is held here or at Weaver. That's what we'll do then.'

Birdswood was not a 'regulating' signal box like Weaver Junction, but Mr Culshaw was very astute when it came to working out how trains ought to proceed. So were his colleagues in the next box at Weaver Junction, come to that, because it was very rare for them to be caught out by giving precedence to a train that would subsequently slow down or hinder in any way a following one. All being well, if our 'coal-mining' was carried out smartly, Weaver Junction would not be any the wiser.

Just as this was going through my mind, Mr Culshaw said, 'What we'll do, Pete, is this. When Sutton Weaver offers us this light engine, you can acknowledge it and give Line Clear so that Johnny [John Boler, the Sutton Weaver signalman] can pull off for it, but we'll wait until just after we get 'Train Entering Section' from him before we offer it forward to Weaver. That way, they'll not expect to see it for about 6 more minutes, and we'll not pull off our Distant so he'll come almost to a stand at our Home signal, then you pull it off slowly and I'll show a red flag from the window. The driver will then creep down to us and stop outside the box.'

'You've got it all worked out so well,' I replied, and recall thinking that I should have known he would have looked at it from all angles before suggesting it.

'When you've been doing it as long as me, Pete, you'll know all the wrinkles. I'm not worried about getting coal for keeping warm, but how else could we boil water for tea?' He beamed his smile at me as if I knew just how much he valued his cups of tea – for that matter, so did I. Anything necessary to prevent that refreshment being curtailed must be worth the effort.

This discussion about obtaining coal started when we began drinking our tea around the time the Saturdays-only Euston-Blackpool train came through at around a quarter to three, and continued in between trains until the final plan was established. In the meantime we had handled the up 'Royal Scot', the down Class H Crewe-Bamfurlong goods, the up Glasgow-Euston, which always followed 6 minutes behind the 'Royal Scot', the down 'Red Rose' Euston-Liverpool Lime Street, and the 8.55am Perth-Euston. The drink of tea had long been finished and the kettle put on the stove again ready for the next one when – not entirely unanticipated – we received a 2-3 bell signal from Sutton Weaver. At last our 'victim' was drawing closer and we could put our plan into operation.

We dealt with this movement in just the same manner as any other, except that our obtaining release from Weaver Junction to unlock our signals was held back until we heard the two bells from John Boler, indicating that this light engine was passing his box and was about to enter our section. Once having offered the 2-3 to Weaver Junction there was – as usual – no delay in it being acknowledged, but I did not pull off any signals. The light engine driver would have seen our colour-light Distant at amber, warning him to be prepared to stop at the Up Home signal. As that signal came into his view, as he continued down the incline and around the corner, he would have realised that something unusual was happening. Little

did he know at that stage that we only wanted to stop him for some coal!

It was very unusual for us at Birdswood not to pull off the up Liverpool Distant, with the result that trains on that track would come down the hill from Sutton Weaver at quite a rate of knots. They had to slow for the permanent speed restriction of 65mph on the curve directly after the flyover just past the box, and the vibrations would rattle the signal box windows as the trains passed just a few feet away on their way south. So when the light engine – a Stanier 'Black Five' – was seen slowly approaching around the curve leading to the up Liverpool Home signal, it was time for action stations.

'I'll tell you when to pull off, Pete, because I want it to come almost to a stand at the signal. The driver will probably guess that something unusual is going on to be stopped here rather than at Weaver Junction. Wait a bit … just another few seconds … there, now pull off.' Just as he said that, the driver gave a 'crow' on his whistle to let us know of his presence in case we had not been watching his approach.

I pulled off the Home signal very slowly, and if the driver had been watching he would immediately guess that something odd was happening and would stop at the box anyway, but just to be sure Mr Culshaw went to the window and displayed the red flag for the driver to see. The engine slowly rolled down the 1 in 415 gradient towards the signal box as Mr Culshaw opened the door and stood on the landing at the top of the steps in order to talk to the driver.

'What's going on, Bobby?' the driver enquired. 'I thought we'd have a clear run at this time of day.'

'Sorry, Driver,' apologised Mr Culshaw, 'but I wondered if you could do me a favour.'

'Aye, if I can – is there something wrong?' he asked.

'Not exactly wrong, but we're in a bit of a state with no coal for the stove to boil the kettle. Could you let us have a bit of yours just to put us on until our delivery?'

As this was being said, I saw the driver's puzzled expression clear from his face as he broke into a wry smile and said, 'Aye, you can

'Black Five' No 44865 coasts downhill from Sutton Weaver on the up Liverpool line towards Birdswood with a partly fitted freight running under bell code 1-2-2, and in about 60 seconds will be rattling the signal box windows. It was from an engine of this class – though not half so clean – that I scavenged coal for the signal box stove. The date is unknown, but judging from the way the locomotive is turned out and the absence of any electrification equipment alongside the track, is likely to be around the mid-1950s. *Author's collection*

have some of this,' pointing back at his tender, 'but you'll have to send your lad up to throw it off.' It was then that I noticed that the tender was piled high with coal, just as if it was about to begin a long-distance run.

'Come on, Pete, jump to it,' said Mr Culshaw. 'We can't delay our friend too long.'

By this time the face of the fireman had appeared at the cab step, and he was laughing as he said, 'The easiest way is up the footsteps at the back of the tender, lad.'

Thinking about it as I sped down the signal box steps, I realised it would have been quite hard – if not impossible – to scramble up the sloping face of the coal in the tender, which would have made a mess on the footplate into the bargain. Not wanting to clear up after such an attempt, the fireman suggested the other approach. Conveniently there were two steps at low level on the side at the back left corner of the tender and a handrail above them to

assist in climbing up Once up at frame level, the footsteps were 'round the corner' on the back left of the tender, and from there I was able to reach the rim at the top of the tank and hold on to that as I climbed the three steps at the back. The next hurdle when standing on the cut-down section of the tender was to clamber over the bulkhead at the back of the coal space in order to handle the lumps I was about to throw down. I remember thinking to myself, 'Why would an engine going into the workshops have its bunker filled so full?' The answer had to be that someone at Edge Hill had made a little mistake.

I had never realised just how large some of the lumps of coal were until that moment, which explained why – when in later years reading about a fireman's experiences on the footplate – there had been mention of breaking up lumps of coal before shovelling them into the firebox. The ones I could lift without straining I hurled over the tender side into our coal bunker, which at this stage of the winter contained only coal dust, hence the need for this escapade. You can well imagine the cloud of coal dust created when each lump landed on the bunker floor, having fallen about 13 feet. Add to that the fact that even before starting to touch the coal I was very grubby indeed from my clambering up the steps of the tender and touching the oily coal dust sticking to its metalwork. I remember that I was wearing yellow socks that day – all the rage in the early 1950s – and a pair of light grey flannels, so in the couple of minutes or so that I was on the tender my appearance was transformed from a clean and tidy youth into something that must have resembled a coalman.

After throwing down about ten or a dozen lumps, which took not much more than a minute, Mr Culshaw called to me that I had thrown off enough, so I made haste to scramble off the tender so as not to delay the engine crew any further. Mr Culshaw had gone back into the box to remove the red flag from the window and came back to the top of the steps to thank the driver just as I walked round the back of the tender to the bottom of the steps. The fireman was staring at me just as I began to mount the steps to the signal box, then he called out, 'By 'eck, lad, you look a bit different now you've done that little job!' I can only assume he was referring to the fact that I was now covered – head to foot – in coal dust, which very likely made me look something akin to a black minstrel. I don't recall making any reply, as by this time the engine had begun rolling forward to continue its journey.

'Before you come back up, Pete,' Mr Culshaw said, 'why don't you break up a few of those lumps and bring up a bucketful while you're still mucky?' Obligingly I did so, and was thinking all the time that I should be very glad to wash off as much of this coal dust as I could. How could I even think of touching the block instruments or levers in this filthy state? This final coal-related task took me a few minutes, but before I had finished I heard Mr Culshaw's voice, but he wasn't talking to me. As I looked up, I saw this lovely girl standing

alongside the up Liverpool track, smiling up at Mr Culshaw who was standing at the top of the steps.

'Have you met Peter Haddock before?' he asked, as he directed her attention to me standing in all my coal dust in the bunker at the foot of the steps.

'No,' she replied.

'This is Joan Hazlehurst from the village,' he said.

I don't know who was most embarrassed, because Joan turned a rather delicate shade of pink while I felt myself blushing to what must have been a very deep pink, which was thankfully hidden by all the coal dust. With his typical chivalry Mr Culshaw invited Joan into the box for a cup of tea, and I am not sure even to this day whether I was relieved that she declined the offer, saying she had to get back home to do something, or disappointed that she was going. Yet how would I have been able to face her in my untidy state? On the other hand, I would have relished the chance of getting to know a bit more about this lovely girl. As it turned out, I gave all my immediate attention to removing the coal dust as best I could before resuming signalling operations.

For the rest of that afternoon I could not get the picture of her lovely face out of my mind. I must have been working on 'auto-pilot' as I went about the job, listening to Mr Culshaw telling me all about her family. He said her Granny ran the Post Office, shop and 'Anvil Café' in the village, her father owned the Smithy Garage and a haulage business, her uncle farmed Smithy Farm, and much of the land on the Dutton village side of the line was owned by the Hazlehurst family. Then, apparently as an after-thought, almost as if to avoid giving the impression that his opinions might have been in some way flavoured by the family's wealth, he said, 'And she's a lovely girl, Pete, don't you think?' I certainly did, and I think for me it must have been love at first sight because I was not at all influenced in my opinion of Joan by whatever her family owned. Had she been the ragged offspring of the poorest family in the area, I would still have been entranced by her lovely serenity and most beautiful smile, despite all my coal dust.

I'm sure that all the trains ran themselves for the rest of that memorable afternoon – 18 April 1953 – and as I left the box to cycle home for a rather late tea I remember deciding that I would certainly write to Joan and invite her to the cinema in Warrington next Saturday evening, because after all I would not be going to Birdswood again for three weeks. Saturday morning the following week would have been an opportunity, as Mr Culshaw would be working the 6-to-2 turn, but I would not be able to visit the box as I played in goal for the village football team and we had an away fixture at Acton Bridge, so I would be leaving on the coach shortly after midday.

That evening was spent thinking about writing and rewriting the letter – to the address in Northwich Road that Mr Culshaw had kindly provided – and I wondered how different the day, or indeed my whole life, would have turned out if I had not climbed up on the tender of a Black Five to hurl lumps of coal into the signal box fuel bunker.

Left Joan, photographed about a year after we met. I don't know what attracted her to a smutty faced youth with coal dust all over his clothes! *Author*

Below This is how both Birdswood and Joan look today, viewed from the quiet comfort of a Liverpool Lime Street to London Euston 'Pendolino' as it passes the site of the signal box on Wednesday 7 July 2004. Note the sub-station built on my favourite trainspotting site! *Author*

11
WORKING FOR A LIVING

It was only during the late 1940s that the school-leaving age in Britain was raised from 14 to 15, and my sister Joan – three years and one month older than me – was among the first to be affected by this change. Although I had some four years to get used to the idea of attending school for an extra year, it caused me no loss of sleep because it was so far into the future. These thoughts make me realise how different things are in schools today; for a few years prior to leaving, my two eldest grandsons were guided through the latter two or three years of their basic schooling by the 'careers officer'. In my time I recall nothing of a careers officer as such, only a visit to the school a few weeks prior to my leaving by a man from the local education office. It was announced in class the day before that he would be coming, and that he would interview each of us to establish where we would go to start working for a living.

The actual interview questions I was asked have faded into the mists of time, but I do recall that there were not many. The man conducting the interview had with him a list of work vacancies in the area, and after a very short time he came to the conclusion that I would probably be suited to engineering and would start an engineering apprenticeship with ICI at its works at Rocksavage. This decision – by him, I must add – was made after only a few minutes, and I feel sure that had he asked me about my hobbies, he would have come to realise that I had more than a passing interest in the railway, but perhaps his list did

not show any vacancies there. Nevertheless I am not unhappy about the career into which I was launched because it proved to be beneficial to me over the rest of my working life. The precision and methods in mechanical engineering, together with many years of academic studies, gave me a fine basis for dealing with matters outside the broad scope of engineering during certain parts of my working life, but I cannot help wondering how different my life would have been had that 'careers officer' asked me about my links with the railway.

My parents were very pleased that I should be directed towards a career with ICI, and in due course all the appropriate arrangements were made following an interview with the Personnel Officer at the Rocksavage works. As the apprenticeship could not commence until I reached my 16th birthday, I would spend almost a year until then in the main engineering workshop at the factory. During this first year I would spend some weeks at the ICI Apprentice Training School in Widnes, where I would be assessed as a result of many aptitude tests, then directed into the most suitable trade.

While all these arrangements were being dealt with, I still of course paid my Saturday afternoon visits to the signal box at Birdswood when Mr Culshaw was on the 2-to-10 shift. During the course of our conversation, in which we would catch up on each other's activities since we were together last, I mentioned that when I left school I would be starting work with ICI. Thinking back to that day, I now realise why Mr Culshaw was less enthusiastic about my future career than I expected him to be. He had been secretly hoping – even expecting – that I would start working for the railway and train to be a signalman, especially after all the training he had given me. He must have been more than a little disappointed that his protégé was to embark upon a career away from British Railways, yet he never let it show in either his words or his actions. The one and only indication of how he must have felt was that he seemed just a little quieter than usual, though that did not register with me at the time. I was totally insensitive to how my news would affect him, and he for his part made an excellent job of hiding his feelings, but continued to coach me in the intricacies of signalling just as he had always done. On reflection, I believe he would have made a better job of guiding me into work than the so-called careers officer, due to the fact that he had tuned right into my interest in the railway. But my working life was to commence elsewhere, and as neither of us could do anything to alter matters, we both carried on as though the arrangements had not been made.

Leaving school was a significant landmark in those days, mainly because it was not until a boy had actually left school that he began to wear long trousers, thus giving an indication of his status to the whole community. My memory tells me that there were one or two of my school pals who began wearing 'long 'uns' while they were still at school, and I recall being allowed to wear mine before leaving school, but only on my visit every third Saturday afternoon to Birdswood signal box. That made me feel really good, because when I wore the railway waistcoat I could stand at the box window to watch passing trains and no one travelling on the train would know that I was a trespasser, whereas with short trousers it was an instant giveaway.

Things linked to my leaving school worked out really well, because my last day as a pupil was the day school broke up for the Easter holiday, whereas my first day as a working 'man' was not until a week the following Tuesday, since the Monday of that week was a bank holiday. As things worked out, that week in between coincided with Mr Culshaw's morning shift – 6.00am until 2.00pm – so I was able to spend a couple of days with him from about half past eight until just before his shift finished. As already mentioned, I had to be out of the box before Ernie Antrobus turned up to take over, because it would not be proper for me to be seen trespassing. Mr Antrobus always arrived in the box 5 minutes before the start of his turn of duty, and if I watched from the booking desk (where most but not quite all of the window was obscured by the panel carrying the telephones) I could see him cycling down the boat road to the stable where he kept his bicycle. Even if he looked towards the box from there, he would not be able to see me, so while he was busy securing his bike inside the stable near the canal tunnel, I would quietly leave the box, cross the main lines and take up my usual trainspotting position on the railway fence opposite the signal box. Then, when I saw him walking up the path towards the box, I would mount my cycle and start the 4-mile ride home.

When Mr Culshaw and I had been arranging my holiday visits, he pointed out that I must not expect to be allowed into the signal box on Mondays, because it was the practice of the ganger, Jim Faulkner, to visit the box as part of his routine during that morning. Neither would I be allowed in on Friday morning for two very good reasons. First, it was almost routine for the Preston Brook Station Master to ride in the brake-van of the pick-up goods to bring wages for the three regular signalmen. Just occasionally, though, he might make the journey on his bike – to catch the duty signalman unawares, perhaps – knowing that if he travelled by the pick-up goods his approach would be heralded by the bell code 2-2-3 ('Freight, ballast or Officers' Special train, requiring to stop in section'), and his visit would therefore not surprise the man on duty. Sometimes this train would have to set back into the refuge siding at Birdswood if a train of more importance was following behind. The second good reason why my visit could not be on

Stanier 'Pacific' No 46243 *City of Lancaster* powers the down 'Mid-day Scot' under the flyover and past the signal box on Saturday 23 July 1955. If the camera was some 15 feet higher, this is more or less the view that could be seen from the box window. *J. A. Peden*

Friday morning was due to the lampman making his weekly visit to replenish the paraffin oil in the signal lamps, and – if he did his job properly – to trim all the wicks.

That week my visits were limited to Tuesday, Wednesday and Thursday, which enabled me to enjoy dealing with the usual weekday traffic rather than the Saturday trains. However, operating the box was just as exciting to me, whether it was for an named express or a slow goods, because the sequence of events was pretty much the same, only the bell code differed. Now that I was not trainspotting but – more importantly – involved with train operation, I was not overly concerned about the class of train, though I must say that on the one occasion I was in the box when the Royal Train passed along the down main line; it was a thrill to signal it by the special 4-4-4 bell code and pull off the down main signals to allow it unhindered passage through the section.

Mr Culshaw was well aware that the local permanent way gang would be involved all the week with some sleeper replacements at Preston Brook goods yard, so the chances of one of the men suddenly visiting the box and finding me there would be very remote. Their daily track inspection would have been carried out first thing in the morning, so by the time I arrived at Birdswood the whole gang would be out of the way. So it was that I thoroughly enjoyed three consecutive morning shifts, or, more precisely, part shifts. Being in that signal box with its colourful levers, polished handles, shiny floor and ringing bells seemed almost a million miles away from the Rocksavage factory where I would soon be starting my working life.

The details of my working life are not of any great importance, especially as they were completely divorced from any matters relating to railways. Yet that is not strictly true, because I recall during my induction tour of Rocksavage Works being pleasantly surprised to find two lines of track running from one end of the site to the other, with several sidings on which chemical tankers were parked for loading. At one point on this tour I heard the unmistakable sound of buffers contacting buffers. Then I saw it! Looking truly resplendent in maroon livery was an 0-4-0 saddle-tank shunting locomotive with what appeared to be over-sized buffers. It was only later that I learned the buffer diameter was large to prevent the buffers locking on some of

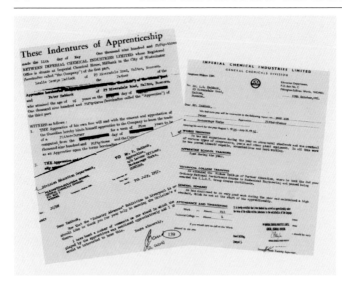

Left Indentures and other papers indicating the interest shown by ICI in the development of its apprentices. *Author*

Below The 0-4-0 saddle-tank shunting locomotive at ICI's Rocksavage Works was built by Andrew Barclay, and could be seen throughout the day bringing empty tankers to be filled or taking away full ones from the various plants in the factory. I had to do some work on it on one occasion while working with the Services Section. The driver was Frank Arrowsmith, a Widnes man who always wore wooden clogs. Shunter and deputy driver Harry Mercer is on the step, while John Dunbabin, also a shunter, stands alongside in this 1953 photograph. *ICI Ltd*

the tight curves the diminutive engine had to negotiate within the factory. This little workhorse was used to shunt within the factory and, if the train formed by the end of the day was not too heavy, to haul it the mile or so along the bank of the Weaver Navigation westwards into the adjacent ICI Castner-Kellner factory at Weston Point. The tank wagons would there be formed into a train that would be taken to Folly Lane Sidings from where – usually during the evening – it would join the national railway network at Runcorn. So clearly I would have the pleasure of seeing trains even when at work.

During the late summer of 1952 I had to attend the ICI Apprentice Training School at Pilkington-Sullivan Works on the eastern outskirts of Widnes for a course to assess aptitude and ability in order to determine which apprenticeship I was to be offered. As things turned out, I was to be trained as a fitter-turner, and shortly after my 16th birthday I would spend seven months at the school being taught the basics. The reason I mention these trips to Widnes is that there ICI had not one but three shunters, not the same design as the one at Rocksavage. They were 0-4-0 saddle-tanks named *Osprey*, *Falcon* and *Kestrel*. In addition to all this, right outside the factory gate was a level crossing and signal box designated Tanhouse Lane Crossing on the LMS line from Warrington to Garston. Perhaps it was fortunate that a tall red-brick wall separated the LMS lines from the tracks within the factory, otherwise I may well have spent time while in the upstairs classroom gazing out of the window rather that concentrating on the instruction from Mr Poole or Mr Ellis. It was distracting enough just having the works shunters back and forth along the factory track. All of this could perhaps be viewed as some form of compensation for having been directed into engineering rather than onto the railway.

In order to get to the training school I opted to cycle the 5 miles or so rather than use public transport. Not only would the latter have been expensive and time-consuming, but it would have involved three separate bus journeys and a ride on the Transporter Bridge in order to cross the River Mersey and the Manchester Ship Canal.

The Transporter was a suspension bridge of 1,100-foot span with a platform hanging from a carriage that traversed along the high-level girder. About 30 feet wide and 80 feet long, the platform had a long covered cabin for passengers on the west side, while vehicles were driven on to the open platform and prevented from rolling off into the water only by the effectiveness of their handbrakes! The carriage was drawn back and forth across the

The author at one of the small lathes in the main workshop at Rocksavage Works during the summer of 1953 shortly after starting his engineering apprenticeship with ICI. *Author's collection*

waters by a cable driven from the winding house on the Widnes side of the Mersey.

I could have crossed over from Cheshire into Lancashire (Widnes was in that county until 1974) with my bicycle using the Transporter, but that could cause some delay as there were only three crossings an hour from each side. The alternative was to cycle across the 'Old Bridge', as the adjacent railway bridge was called. Despite having to ride up the steeply sloping wooden ramp, then carry my cycle up 42 steps to reach the narrow path alongside the railway, I much preferred this route simply because it was so close to the main Euston to Liverpool line. There were

No 46207 *Princess Arthur of Connaught* brings the up 'Merseyside Express' across Runcorn Bridge on Saturday 8 August 1959. M. *Walshaw*

many times during my use of this path that – on hearing the sound of an approaching train – I would stop to lean on the wall to watch the train pass by just beyond the end of my nose. I contend that apart from standing on a station platform, one could not legally get closer to a train. An excellent view of passing rail traffic could be enjoyed while using the parts of the path on the stone viaducts at either end, as can be seen from the accompanying photograph, but any trains passing while I was cycling along the centre sections, where the lattice girders were carried on the huge sandstone piers, would be pretty well obscured by the ironwork.

All of this detail tends to strengthen my links with railway matters, despite now working outside the industry. I really did enjoy working for ICI, as they really looked after their employees and I learned such a lot apart from all the many technicalities of my apprenticeship and my studies of engineering at night school and on day-release courses. Yet there are even more incidents during the five years I was serving my apprenticeship that brought me into contact with railways. One such occurred in June 1957 when I was selected to be one of the apprentices to help man the company stand at the 'Industry Advances' exhibition in a large hall in Liverpool. Yet it was not just the exhibition itself that delighted me – that was certainly a great privilege – but rather it was the train journeys from Runcorn to Liverpool Lime Street and back, all at the company's expense, for all the days of the exhibition. Those readers who have at some time visited Lime Street in steam days will know what a hive of activity it was there, and I was able to arrive there earlier than necessary during the morning and linger a while at the end of the day in order to soak up that busy atmosphere. It was especially important to me to witness the departure for Euston at 5.25pm of the one-stop express 'The Red Rose', usually hauled by a gleaming 'Princess Royal' Class engine, which would whisk the prestige train to Platform 1 at Euston by 9.10pm. Once that had departed I would catch the Chester train to Runcorn after noting down the numbers of a few engines.

The other railway link to my work came quite unexpectedly during the time I spent working with craftsmen in the works Services Section. I should explain that apprentice engineers spent several six-month periods working on the various chemical plants, as opposed to being in the main workshop, in order to gain valuable experience dealing with machinery overhauls and suchlike. One of those periods was spent with the Services Section responsible for the maintenance of the boiler house, steam distribution system, water treatment and filtration systems and other such things. Included in all of this were the day-to-day minor repairs to the works shunting locomotive. All major repair works were undertaken elsewhere, but I once had the privilege of spending almost a whole day under the guidance of a fitter named Jim Rowlands attending to a faulty injector, sanding gear problems and replacing a water-level gauge glass. I vividly recall spending most of my lunch break on the footplate, almost daring myself to release the brake and open the throttle. At that time I knew nothing of the damage one could cause by not opening the cylinder drain cocks before opening the throttle, so it is a good job I didn't rise to my own challenge of trying to move the loco!

During the earlier part of my apprenticeship I visited Mr Culshaw at Birdswood signal box whenever I knew he was on duty, and it was during that time that the events related in Chapter 1 took place. In fact, I spent several Friday night to Saturday morning shifts working the box. That enabled me to make sufficient recovery over the weekend to be fit for ICI work again on Monday morning.

During the initial years of my working life my association with railways as a direct consequence of work – already explained in this chapter – were somewhat tenuous, but by some strange coincidence I came to have an almost daily connection with railways during the last few years of my working life. It all came about as a result of my wish to become self-employed in order to free up some time for important voluntary activities in which I was deeply involved. I worked in the technical services department of a local authority supervising the administration of the many and varied engineering functions, and during the mid-1980s, when I wished to move into part-time work, job-sharing had not yet been introduced. I was thus forced to resign, as my post – it was argued – could not be satisfied on a part-time basis.

Giving up an interesting and well-paid job with its pension was not easy, but my voluntary work was more important, so in order to earn something of a living I became involved in doing building repairs, kitchen and bathroom refurbishments, and even some window cleaning. In fact, this latter activity soon became established as my main occupation. However, as I entered my early 60s I came to realise that such work was more suited to younger men, so I began looking for something I would find less taxing.

By this time I was living in Wiltshire where a friend of mine worked as a cleaner for a commercial vehicle leasing company. He would often tell me of being called upon to leave the cleaning and drive a new truck to some distant part of the country, from where he would return by train. I love driving, especially trucks, and I love even more travelling by train, and when he told me the company wished to take on a part-time driver, I went for an interview. It was conducted by the Operations Manager, who told me that the company had two directors and 20 employees, and owned 600 vehicles of varying types at many locations throughout the country. He took me through a driving test on three different sizes of trucks, and a couple of days later I received a letter confirming my appointment.

At first I ran the driving work in tandem

My driving job involved a fair amount of train travel the length and breadth of Britain. This is Totnes, where the former signal box on the up platform has been thoughtfully converted to serve as a café. I sampled the coffee there on Monday 20 March 2000. *Author*

The Liverpool-Penzance service on Wednesday 7 August 2002 is formed by Class 221 'Super Voyager' No 221129 *George Vancouver*, on which I enjoyed an exhilarating journey as far as Bristol. *Author*

My first ride on an 'Adelante' was a short hop on this one, No 180112, from Bath Spa to Temple Meads on Friday 4 October 2002. My onward journey to St Austell was aboard a First Great Western HST. *Author*

Having ridden this 'Super Voyager', No 221111 *Roald Amundsen*, from Bristol Temple Meads, I was about to make my first journey into Cornwall courtesy of a Wessex Trains Class 153. The date is Monday 30 September 2002. *Author*

with window cleaning, but it was not too long before the excitement of all the rail travel overpowered the boredom of window cleaning, so I fixed my full attention on the driving job. In some cases the driving came first, as when a new truck was to be delivered to a customer, then the train journey would follow, and almost always involved a change of trains so that some time could be spent watching what was going on at the station and, whenever there was anything of interest, taking photographs. There were other occasions, however, when the train journey came first, which meant that I could properly plan my journey, but I must admit that it was not quite as exciting as returning to base by train, because much would depend upon when I arrived at the destination and how frequently the trains operated. It was sometimes more than a little exciting, not knowing which route to take home. These travels took me onto all the UK franchises except Scotrail and Island Line, the former because one leg of the journey to or from Scotland would be by air, and the latter because we only had one small customer on the Isle of Wight.

My very first outward journey by rail was on Monday 5 July 1999, when I was to collect a 5-ton Iveco van from the Priestman Works on the eastern outskirts of Hull where it had been fitted with a hydraulic access platform, known as a 'cherry-picker'. That day my train journey began on the 0706 Wales & West service from Trowbridge to Bristol Temple Meads. A short wait gave me time enough to buy a coffee before boarding the 0757 Virgin Cross Country service to Birmingham New Street. Changing from the Glasgow-bound High Speed Train to catch the 1000 Virgin

Newcastle service as far as Sheffield Midland, I came to realise that this particular train from Plymouth had left Temple Meads at 0830, so I could have boarded it there and avoided the gloomy change at New Street. I later came to realise that I could just as well have changed trains at Doncaster, which I did on subsequent journeys and was able to photograph some action on the East Coast Main Line. At Sheffield I boarded the Northern Spirit service for Hull, where we arrived – after a more than lively journey in the Class 142 'Pacer' – 3 minutes before the scheduled time. Met at the station by a member of the Priestman team, the drive to their works took us past the Humbrol and Airfix factory where a real Hawker Hunter jet aircraft was displayed on a pedestal on the front lawn.

I made that journey on several different occasions, either to deliver new vehicles to Priestmans or to collect and bring back modified ones. Those trips gave me the opportunity to change trains at various places to take photographs, some of which are included here. One of the journeys I most enjoyed, and which I made fairly often, was to St Austell in Cornwall. Not only was the trip along the Dawlish sea wall in a 'Super Voyager' a memorable experience, but so was crossing the River Tamar at 15mph by Brunel's famous Royal Albert Bridge at Saltash. By contrast, I once made the Plymouth to St Austell sector in a run-down Class 153, something I can't generate very much enthusiasm about but which was, when all is said and done, a part of my overall travel experience.

Since this chapter is all about working for a living, that was not a bad way to do it, don't you think?

12
WHEN THINGS WENT WRONG

It should not be at all surprising that, covering a period of more than 150 years over the almost 50 track miles of railway featured in this book, some form of accident should have occurred to upset the otherwise smooth running of the railway in this area. Considering the fact that there are four main-line junctions, two tunnels, one level crossing and a fairly stiff gradient with catch points, the surprise might well be that there have been so few accidents at all. Add to this the number of train movements in the average 24-hour period – more than 300 – and the full picture begins to emerge that this part of the railway world has had its full quota of good fortune.

However, it goes without saying that such accident-free working depends upon many different things, not least of which is the dedication and attention to details of hundreds – perhaps thousands – of railwaymen (and these days women) who have carried out their daily duties with a great deal of skill and pride. Nevertheless, it only takes one small mistake, perhaps a flawed judgement, maybe a momentary loss of concentration or possibly the effect of working under extreme pressure, to plunge the whole operation into disaster.

There can be no doubt that dealing with many excursion trains in addition to the average daily scheduled trains does create such pressure. This is apparent not only at management level, where every arrangement has to be carefully dovetailed into the standard pattern of operations, but also out on the ground where train crews, platform staff and signalmen all have that extra workload with which to contend.

SUTTON TUNNEL: 30 APRIL 1851

Such was the situation more 150 years ago on 30 April 1851 when the newly formed Birkenhead, Lancashire & Cheshire Junction Railway laid on many excursion trains to convey horse-racing enthusiasts from various locations in south Lancashire and north Cheshire to the county town of Chester to witness the series of events linked with the Chester Cup held on the Roodee, a splendid course located just outside the city walls on a bend in the banks of the River Dee. In those days the weather was perhaps more predictable and reliable than in our time, and no doubt there was something of a festive atmosphere permeating Chester on that day. Much money will have been lost and won, the racegoers will have been dressed in all their finery, and after the excitement of that race meeting it can well be imagined that those returning from Chester by train would have settled back into their seats to meditate upon the activities of the day, to gloat over the amount of money won, or perhaps to formulate some excuse to offer those at home as to why the pocket-book was now so much slimmer than first thing that morning!

The railway company coped extremely well

with the nearly 10,000 passengers who presented themselves for travel at the end of that afternoon. Since the Birkenhead, Lancashire & Cheshire Junction Railway was a relatively new organisation (weren't they all in those days?), with its line between Chester and Walton Junction, near Warrington, having been open for traffic only since the previous 18 December, most if not all of the railwaymen involved were under some pressure to handle the great influx of extra passengers. Remember that this may well have been the first time they had dealt with such passenger numbers. Why, even today that figure would create more than a few headaches for the staff involved. So the fact that they managed to get all the passengers aboard the right trains within a very short space of time says much for their training and abilities.

One can visualise a procession of seven excursion trains, all heading away from Chester along the new line towards Warrington with short time intervals between them. How exciting it must have been for small boys (and their fathers) seeing so much traffic on an otherwise fairly quiet line of railway. Such a fine procession must have been a wonderful sight, no doubt including products of the recently opened Crewe locomotive works not far away. More than likely the locomotives would have been single-wheelers without the luxury of a cab for the footplate crew, hauling their trains of assorted four-wheeled coaches, some of which may have been of the earliest design, thus offering little if any protection from the elements.

At that time trains were 'controlled' by the time-interval method, by which a train would not be dispatched by the station master until a certain period had elapsed. The time interval would have been determined beforehand, having regard for the terrain, gradients and curves of the line, and so on. If a train ran well, it would have been held at the next station until the time-interval had passed to ensure its separation from the preceding train, thus ensuring safety.

Almost 12 miles east from Chester along this new line was Sutton Tunnel, 1 mile 176 yards long, and about 4½ miles before the

point where the line joined the Grand Junction Railway just south of Warrington. A station was located at Frodsham, about 2 miles west of the tunnel, and it fell to the lot of the station master there to regulate the onward movement of this convoy of excursion traffic. From Frodsham the line was on a mainly rising gradient for eastbound trains, climbing at 1 in 264 into the tunnel and reaching the summit about halfway through. The only respite on this climb was a mile or so after Frodsham station where an embankment and viaduct carried the line on the level over the River Weaver and the Weaver Navigation.

One of the early trains in the series of specials leaving Frodsham station found the uphill gradient more than a match for its power and consequently it stalled before reaching the western portal of Sutton Tunnel. The line from Frodsham station to the tunnel was virtually straight, which is just as well because the driver of the next train, given 'right away' from Frodsham, must have seen the earlier train at a stand ahead of him. When he brought his train safely to a stop behind the stalled train, it was decided by the crews involved that the second train would buffer up to the stalled train to help it forward, thus clearing the way for the several other excursion trains that they knew would be following at close intervals behind.

It is always much easier with hindsight to decide what course of action would have been for the best. There is no doubt that for an already fully laden train to attempt to assist another equally heavily loaded excursion on a fairly stiff rising gradient into a dark tunnel could only be described as foolhardy, but remember that all these railway servants were struggling under the great pressure of an expanded timetable for the Chester Races. If you had been on the spot at that time, what would you have done? What options were there available?

Though it would have taken much more time, perhaps it would have been better for the first train to detach a few carriages and proceed to Warrington with a shorter train, returning for the remainder later. That would undoubtedly have kept the line blocked for at least half an hour as well as creating a major headache operationally as to where the returning locomotive could cross over to the original line, as well as requiring someone to give authority for a length of 'wrong-line' working. So perhaps we should not be surprised that the train crews involved took the action they did, very likely having given careful consideration to the options, with the time delay influencing their decision.

This double-length train began to move slowly forward, helped by the fact that the stalled locomotive had, in the meantime, built up a greater head of steam and was better placed to cope with its heavy load. Who knows – but for the assistance of the second train, it may not have been able to start away on the uphill slope. However, start it did, and the mouth of Sutton Tunnel gradually came nearer and nearer until eventually the combined length of the two trains disappeared into the darkness. A minute or two later they were defeated by the gradient once more and stalled. The following train, with a more powerful engine or a lighter load – or both – was waved away by the Frodsham station master after the lapse of the appropriate interval, and sped into the tunnel. The footplate crew were totally unaware of the two stalled trains ahead of them in the pitch blackness. All was now set in place for what could only result in a major catastrophe.

What must the passengers in those trains have felt when they realised that the following express was bearing down upon them at speed? What could they do? Where could they go? Was there anywhere they could flee in order to avoid being run down by the speeding express? The answer of course to all those questions was 'No'. In the resulting carnage six people lost their lives, with a great number of others being seriously injured, and though their injuries did in time heal, many of them must have later gone to their graves with the horror of that moment engraved upon their minds. The only wonder is that not more passengers were killed.

Two factors were brought into play that prevented that horrific catastrophe being compounded. First, there was no traffic in the opposite direction – if there had been it would have added to an already serious accident.

Second, the guard of the third train immediately carried out the urgent duty of protecting his train by running back along the line with a lighted handlamp to warn the next train to stop.

Such a tragedy as this during the infancy of passenger railways must have disheartened those who believed that the railway would be the modern means of speedy and safe travel for those who, hitherto, had been obliged to make any lengthy journey by stagecoach. As far as I can ascertain in my research, this was the country's first fatal railway accident within a tunnel, though it was by no means the first where an underpowered or overloaded train had stalled and been run into by the one following. There must have been innumerable lessons learned from the Sutton Tunnel disaster, but unfortunately those lessons did not prevent further such accidents from marring the safety record of the railway companies concerned. It was to be some years before any positive improvements to train safety were made.

WEAVER JUNCTION: TUESDAY 14 JANUARY 1930

While not involving any fatalities or indeed injuries of any kind, an accident involving the down 'Mid-day Scot' at this flying junction created something of a mystery for the investigating officer, the locomotive designers and maintenance personnel. Hauled by one of the fairly new 'Royal Scot' Class locomotives, No 6131 *Planet*, the prestigious Euston to Glasgow express with Driver J. Kay at the controls approached Weaver Junction some 3 minutes late at a speed variously estimated to be between 56 and 70 miles per hour. It there had to negotiate the flying junction on which a speed limit of 55mph had been imposed. The track at this point was rising on a gradient of 1 in 330, with the left-hand rail being superelevated about 3 inches higher than the right in order to assist speeding trains negotiate the slight right-hand curve of 30 chains radius. Check rails were also located at this high-speed junction.

The investigating officer, Colonel

This 1954 photograph clearly shows the 'flying junction' just beyond Weaver Junction signal box, with the points set for the Liverpool branch. No 49282 heads an up freight from Carnforth on Monday 5 April. *Norman Preedy archive*

Anderson, established that the right-hand leading coupled wheel climbed the check rail some 7 feet before reaching the nose of the crossing. As a result, the left-hand leading coupled wheel struck the nose of the crossing, causing it to run along the top of the left-hand rail before dropping outside it, breaking fishplate bolts and chairs in the process. Driver Kay immediately applied the brake and brought his train to a stand some 1,091 yards beyond the point of derailment. All other wheels remained on the rails.

Evidence regarding the works inspection of the locomotive immediately following the accident showed some wear of the tyre profile, especially some 'thinning' of the flange, as well as wear in the axleboxes and horn guides, permitting excessive side play. Colonel Anderson concluded that the accident was caused by a combination of high speed, flange wear, and excessive side play. His belief was that Driver Kay seriously underestimated his speed, which, by the evidence of two platelayers at the scene, was around 70mph, and that he must accept some measure of responsibility for the accident.

Interestingly, Colonel Anderson suggested that consideration be given to increasing the guiding effect of bogies of engines of this class. That suggestion was taken up by the LMS and, as a consequence, firmer side-control springs were fitted to the bogies, with positive results.

MOORE:
FRIDAY 13 MAY 1966

More than 36 years were to elapse before the next serious accident took place on the tracks of this area, and although no passengers lost their lives, there were fatal consequences.

The location was on the outskirts of the village of Moore, where the West Coast Main Line approaches Acton Grange Junction from the south, at which point the LMS&GWR

'Black Five' No 45235 passes Acton Grange Junction with an up passenger train on 5 June 1954. The distinctive girder bridge carries the West Coast Main Line and the Warrington-Chester line over the Manchester Ship Canal. The accident here 12 years later occurred just out of shot to the left. The 1 in 135 gradient is noticeable. *Norman Preedy archive*

Joint line from Chester to Warrington converges from the east (see the map on page 79). The down WCML track runs uphill on a fairly sharp gradient of 1 in 135 here, though down expresses travelling at around 70mph found no difficulty with this incline, artificially created in 1893 to carry the railway over the newly cut Manchester Ship Canal. A distinctive multi-girder bridge is often clearly seen as a distinguishing feature on the many photographs that have been taken at this location.

Late on Friday evening, 13 May 1966, a hopper train conveying soda ash from ICI Northwich to the Pilkington glass factory at St Helens made its way sedately up the incline approaching Acton Grange Junction. The weight of the load and the gradient conspired to reduce the train's speed. However, as the locomotive and the leading part of the train were about to cross the canal at the girder bridge, the guard – Daniel Murphy of Weaverham, near Northwich – felt a thud, which his experience told him meant that a coupling somewhere along his train had broken. This was confirmed right away as the rear of the train quickly slowed to a halt. The 1 in 135 uphill incline at this point caused the rearmost part of the train to begin rolling back, completely out of control, down the

incline and towards any traffic that may have been following it.

Immediately Guard Murphy knew what action he must take. He screwed down the brake of his guard's van to retard this backward movement, but due to the fact that – unknown to him at the time – 23 fully laden wagons had parted from the train, his prompt action proved insufficient to prevent a build-up of speed as this rogue part of the heavy train ran away in the wrong direction. A nightmare scenario had begun to unfold.

In former times, only a few years earlier, when Acton Grange signal box was manned, the signalman would have noticed the train pass without a tail lamp and would have automatically assumed that part of the train had broken away. He would have put into operation the standard procedure for dealing with such an obstruction. In the majority of cases, when a train passed without a tail lamp visible it was simply because it had gone out (they were paraffin lamps in those days) or had not been placed on the last vehicle of the train at the start of the journey. But a signalman cannot assume that to be the case, hence the obstruction procedure. In this case there was indeed such an obstruction – 23 soda-ash hoppers running away on the wrong line.

What could be more of a hazard to a

following express train dashing through the midnight darkness at 60 or 70mph? Yet the fact that the soda-ash train had become divided would not register in the nearby power signal box at Warrington until it ran through the next set of axle-counters, or the signalman noticed that the track circuit for that section of track was still showing an 'occupied' light, despite the fact that the train was some miles ahead. It would seem that such indicators were not noticed, and consequently a tragedy was about to unfold.

Back in the guard's van of the runaway part of the train, Guard Murphy had done everything possible in his attempt to halt the rearward movement of the train, yet it continued to build up speed as it ran back down the incline. He must have known that when his train had been allowed out onto the West Coast Main Line near Acton Bridge (just south of Weaver Junction) it would have had to run well to keep out of the way of any following express. He may even have known that the Stranraer boat train was close on his heels. No doubt he kept a good look-out as his train ran backwards, and it is a good job he did, for he must have seen the marker lights of the diesel-hauled boat train approaching out of the darkness. What a dilemma! If he stayed on board, his guard's van would be smashed to pieces in the inevitable collision and he would

lose his life. Even though the breakaway was now running backwards at a speed he estimated to be approaching 50mph, he jumped clear and thus saved his life.

The 2040 boat train from Euston to Stranraer hauled by diesel-electric engine No D322 was bowling along the down line passing through the block section of the former Birdswood signal box, some 4 miles from Moore. Heading northwards towards Warrington, it is believed that the boat train was brought to a stand at Norton Crossing due to the fact that the preceding soda-ash train had not yet cleared the Acton Grange section. If this is true, then it was – in a sense – fortuitous, because it would otherwise have been travelling much faster by the time it reached Moore. As it was, the boat train moved onward towards disaster. Driver G. Cannon from Penrith depot and Fireman F. Bell of Carlisle Upperby would have been very carefully watching the road, picking out the various signals and any landmarks that would indicate their precise position along this well-used main line.

It can be imagined that, as the train approached Acton Grange Junction, it would not be easy for the driver to spot the tail light on the rogue hoppers, if indeed there was one, because as the bridge over the Manchester Ship Canal was approached there would be a

Clearing up operations at Moore show the breakdown cranes from Edge Hill and Rugby dominating the accident scene, watched by many onlookers including members of the local constabulary. The soda-ash can be seen scattered all over the scene. This accident would have interested people of the nearby village and railway enthusiasts from far and wide. *Harold Dunning*

plethora of variously coloured lights from the town of Warrington just beyond the canal. Even if the driver had seen a tail lamp and had initiated an emergency stop, it clearly was insufficient to prevent his train running headlong into the soda-ash hoppers. At precisely 10 minutes before midnight on that fateful Friday – the 13th – the speeding boat train met head-on with the runaway guard's van and the 23 hoppers connected to it. As a tragic result, the diesel locomotive burst into flames, reared up by the force of the massive impact, and came to rest on top of some of the hoppers. The cab of the locomotive was crushed beyond all recognition, trapping and fatally injuring Driver Cannon and Fireman Bell.

Bearing in mind the fact that D322 was hauling a boat train, it is nothing short of miraculous that not a single passenger among the 100 on board was fatally injured. Catastrophic though the accident was, the most serious injuries sustained were cuts and bruises. It does not bear thinking about what may have resulted if the impact had taken place a little further on, immediately before the canal bridge, more than 75 feet above the water of the chilly Manchester Ship Canal. At the very least, some of the coaches of the boat train would likely have fallen down the high embankment and into the canal, with even more tragic results, almost certainly with some passengers losing their lives.

As it was, it is likely that the tail lamp of the runaway hoppers was spotted by the boat train driver, who made an emergency brake application. Sadly, however, it was nowhere near early enough to prevent a collision, but at least slowed down the train sufficiently to permit the coaches to remain upright.

Clearing up after any railway accident is given the highest priority. In this case, operations were hampered to a large extent by the soda-ash dust being blown about the wreck scene, causing choking and temporary blindness in many of the rescue workers. Medical staff from the nearby ICI works were on hand to help those affected by the chemical and, together with local ambulance crews, gave first aid to the injured passengers.

Several lengths of track where the collision occurred had to be replaced, together with sleepers and ballast, just as soon as the locomotive and wrecked hoppers had been moved away. More permanent way workers were brought in to help clear up around the scene and, despite the carnage caused by this accident, the West Coast Main Line was reopened to traffic at 6.00am on Sunday morning. The whole operation was carried out in just 36 hours! In comparison, how long would such an accident keep the line closed today?

There is one rather unusual detail linked to this tragedy. Owing to the slow rate of progress at cutting away the mass of wreckage of the diesel locomotive in order to extricate the crew trapped inside, it was decided – after special permission had been obtained from the Coroner – to remove the diesel to the workshops at Crewe, where hydraulic and cold-cutting machinery was available. The work of removing twisted metal to get to the bodies of Driver Cannon and Fireman Bell could be carried out more quickly there, so around midnight on Saturday 14 May D322 was moved. It is of some interest to note that the bodies, once they had been recovered from the wrecked cab, were taken to a mortuary in Stockton Heath – near the scene of the disaster – where they were later formally identified.

WEAVER JUNCTION: 6 AUGUST 1975

Had this accident occurred just 20 years earlier, I might well have been a witness to the tragedy. But then the word 'if' can be used in regard to all sorts of circumstances, and the results would have been different. The fact that one type of train involved in this specific accident was not in existence 20 years earlier might well have changed things altogether, so pontificating about 'what ifs' really serves no useful purpose at all. I shall therefore confine myself – for the most part, anyway – to the facts.

Imperial Chemical Industries had several manufacturing plants in the north Cheshire area, all railway-served, and had a large fleet of private-owner vehicles, mainly tanks for the

On Wednesday 5 April 1978 Class 40 diesel-electric locomotive No 40095 leaves the ICI sidings at Runcorn Folly Lane with a train of 45-ton tank wagons transporting caustic soda to the ICI works at Wallerscote, near Northwich. This train is similar in many respects to the one referred to in the text, which came to grief at Weaver Junction some three years earlier. *J. A. Sommerfield*

conveyance of various chemical products. A good deal of inter-factory traffic took place between Runcorn and Northwich, with a regular train of caustic soda tanks identified by the TOPS code 6F52. On 6 August 1975 this train departed from Runcorn Folly Lane sidings at 21.40 behind Class 40 No 40189, made up of 20 tanks each of 45 tons gross laden weight, making a load of some 900 tons, plus the weight of the loco. Unfortunately not all the vehicles were fitted with air brakes, so the running speed of the train should have been reduced from the usual 60mph, since the braking force of the mixed train was something less than a quarter of the total train weight. The alternative would have been for some of the tanks to be detached and a lighter train operated. As it was, only some of the tanks had effective brakes.

This train was routed from Folly Lane sidings at Runcorn onto the up Liverpool main line, travelling thence to join the West Coast Main Line at Weaver Junction. Just over 3 miles later it would diverge to the left between Acton Bridge and Hartford, eventually making its way to the Wallerscote Works on the outskirts of Northwich. That was the plan, but for the moment we shall leave this train at Sutton Weaver as it commences the 1 in 101 downgrade past Birdswood heading for Weaver Junction (by this time Birdswood signal box no longer existed).

Some 4 hours earlier a 75mph Freightliner train, running under TOPS code 4O68, began its journey from Glasgow to Southampton.

Hauled by a Class 81 electric locomotive, the train was made up of 15 container vehicles carrying whisky, mail and an assortment of other goods. It would run southwards along the West Coast Main Line at least as far as Crewe, thereafter continuing under diesel haulage through Stafford, Birmingham, Oxford and Reading, and on to the Southampton Maritime Terminal. Being allowed to run at 75mph meant that by the time our caustic soda train was leaving Runcorn, the Freightliner train would have been approaching Warrington, just a few minutes' running time north of Weaver Junction where – if all went according to plan – it would pass the junction and run onto Dutton Viaduct. The caustic soda train would then join the WCML a few minutes later.

Let us now rejoin the ICI train as it begins the descent from Sutton Weaver, at which point matters began – imperceptibly at first – to run out of control. In order not to exceed what he believed to be the maximum speed for a train such as his, the diesel locomotive driver would have begun applying the brakes soon after starting down the hill. Perhaps it was just a few moments before he realised to his horror that the braking was having little or no effect on the train, and he would likely have then fully applied the brake, hoping to at least keep the speed under the 65mph maximum permitted on the right-hand curve that started at the flyover crossing the West Coast Main Line. Unknown to him, his full brake application was causing sparks to fly – literally – and he would have been more than

Fourteen years before the 'whisky and soda' accident, Signalman Joe Huntbach is seen at the panel in the new signal box at Weaver Junction. *British Railways*

a little concerned, having just passed Weaver Junction's Outer Distant signal at caution, knowing that he was expected to bring his train to a full stop at the Home signal. Clearly he must have recognised that at his present rate of progress such a feat was absolutely impossible. He would become guilty of passing a signal at danger.

His heart must have sank if he, at that moment, had looked to his right to see the Freightliner train passing him at 75mph, at which time both trains were much less than half a mile from the point where the two tracks converged. There was no chance that either train could be brought to a stand before the junction to avoid a collision.

For nearly 15 years by that time, the signalling function at Weaver Junction had been relocated a quarter of a mile further north from where the first signal box had been located immediately to the north of Dutton Viaduct, and a modern box had been built above the relay room on the up side of the tracks. The control of trains was by means of an electronic panel on which the positions of trains was constantly shown. The signalman there must have begun to worry as he realised that the train from Runcorn was not going to stop at the junction. There was little he could do in the few seconds remaining to avert disaster, as there was nowhere he could divert the offending caustic soda train. He must have been horrified at the prospect of a serious collision right in front of his very eyes. Fortunately he had the presence of mind to remember that he had cleared his down

signals for a Liverpool-bound express passenger train. This fast-running train would – if something were not done – plough right into the wreckage resulting from the collision that was about to happen on the opposite track. He therefore replaced the down signals to danger, which, without any shadow of doubt, prevented what in a few seconds would be a disastrous collision from becoming a human tragedy.

Meanwhile the Freightliner driver must have been looking forward to the end of his shift as he came within 16 miles of Crewe with about half an hour of his working day left. Then, as his electric locomotive, running at 75mph under clear signals, passed under the flyover carrying the up Liverpool line over the West Coast Main Line tracks, he must have seen the caustic soda train just ahead and over to his left. Sparks were flying from its wheel rims, a sight that any seasoned railwayman knows indicates that the brakes are not holding the train. The grave situation could only worsen. He must have suddenly felt sick in the pit of his stomach, realising just how close the converging junction was, and that he could not possibly stop in time. The train on his left would simply run into him as both trains met at the junction. What a dilemma!

The Freightliner driver decided that since he could not brake to a stop in time to avert disaster, he would accelerate in the hope that at least his locomotive would reach the junction before the runaway train. It did. Was that decision the result of years of experience, an intuitive reaction, or just the lesser of two evils?

The wreckage at Weaver Junction. The twisted chassis of a freightliner bogie lies across the down track. Note the damaged overhead line equipment, and significant damage has also been caused to the track. Little wonder that it took about a week to sort out the debris, clear the line, readjust the tracks and restore the power system. *BR, Silver Link collection via Brian Grant*

Whatever the answer, it saved his life; had he decided to brake instead, he might well have been crushed to death as his cab would have been flattened on impacting with the heavy caustic soda tanks. Thankfully his locomotive had just crossed the junction a split second before the runaway train ran into the left side of his container train. The diesel locomotive, all the tank wagons in its train and most of the containers in the other train were derailed.

As a result of the collision many of the caustic soda tanks were ruptured and the hazardous contents spilled over a wide area. What liquor remained in the tanks was recovered by being siphoned out into road vehicles. Pools of the substance formed in various parts of the track, thus creating a further hazard to the workers involved in clearing up. Copious amounts of water were hosed over the site to dilute the caustic, but sadly much of it washed down into the River Weaver and adjacent Dutton Flashes (natural shallow pools on the river floodplain), killing all the fish that had recently been introduced. Its effect on the soil of the area can only be imagined!

The overhead line equipment was brought down, with conductors and catenaries becoming entangled in the wreckage. Many of the containers – some of which, you will recall, were loaded with bottled whisky – were split open on impact and their contents strewn all over the scene. There had never been a more macabre meaning to the expression 'whisky and soda'.

For almost a week the West Coast Main Line remained blocked, diversions being arranged via Manchester or Chester. The effects of the spillages had to be neutralised as

best they could, with ICI staff being involved together with many fire service and railway personnel. Since the site was fairly difficult to access (one of the reasons why I have experienced many problems finding more than just a few photographs taken hereabouts) many of the local landowners readily cooperated in allowing their fields and farm tracks adjoining the crash scene to be used. The various difficulties encountered in the clearing-up operation were exacerbated by the extremely hot weather. Many suffered heat exhaustion from having to work in full protective clothing to prevent caustic burns to their skin. Certainly a great disaster, but one that could well have been much, much worse but for some well-experienced railwaymen.

There have been times when things went wrong just outside the area covered by this volume, such as at Winsford in 1948, Coppenhall Junction in 1937, Winwick Junction in 1934, and Walton Junction in 1867, some of which resulted in fatalities. And just in case anyone should begin to think that there appear to have been many accidents in the area, remember that those mentioned in this chapter occurred over a time span of more than 150 years. Yet despite the distinction of having the country's first 'flying junction' installed in 1869 at Weaver Junction there have never been any derailments or other accidents to trains travelling in the down direction, apart from the 1930 derailment mentioned earlier. Quite a feat, considering the fact that trains could – and did – take the junction at speeds of 50mph and on some occasions a little more! A far cry from the days of the stagecoach!

13
THE AREA TODAY

Feeding on one's memories of past good times and sharing reminiscences with someone of like mind can only go on for so long before the realisation of what prevails today is brought fully home. Such has been my experience in writing down events that occurred 50 or more years ago, suddenly becoming very much aware of just how significantly that part of the railway system mentioned in these pages has changed.

The infamous 1955 Modernisation Plan, by which steam was to be eliminated from British Railways, has much to answer for, especially when some serious thought is given to how much more the steam locomotive could have been developed and made more efficient. Yet it must be accepted that perhaps even greater change was brought about by the electrification of the West Coast Main Line, and of course some other parts of the system. Utilising 25kV power supplies was without doubt the watershed leading to faster trains, with today's 'Pendolino' sets capable of more than twice the speed achieved by many express trains fifty years ago. It was this transition to AC electric traction with its overhead line equipment that brought such radical changes to Birdswood and the area around it.

It goes without saying that such things as the rapid growth of lineside vegetation and the abolition of localised gangs of platelayers have had a great impact on the appearance of our railways, because no longer do the lengthmen cut back shrubs and trees, mow down long grass on embankments and in cuttings, and generally keep their section of the track in pristine condition. Even if one cannot imagine the difference these changes have made, one has only to scan the pages of any of the 'past and present'-type books to have the truth of this fact brought home. Not that Birdswood alone has been so changed – it has happened virtually everywhere.

Long before the electrification programme north of Weaver Junction was implemented, plans had been laid to centralise the signalling functions. As far as Birdswood signal box was concerned, it was to be taken out of use soon after the overhead line equipment had been erected over its section. Responsibility for the control of trains passing through the section would be transferred to the newly built Weaver Junction signal box, located above the relay room a few hundred yards north of the Weaver viaduct. Even that was only a temporary measure until the new power signal box at Warrington became fully operational.

The rationale behind this move is not hard to comprehend, because with electrical power and a fleet of brand new locomotives available, train speeds would be higher, making it impractical to have signal boxes a couple of miles or so apart clearing the line for trains to proceed. Not only that, but with electricity now being readily available all along the trackside, colour-light signals would replace the old semaphore arms, some of which had been in use for more than 100 years! Thus each power signal box would

In July 1999 a Virgin High Speed Train hurtles northwards past the site of the former bracket signal and in about 5 minutes will be passing through Warrington Bank Quay station. *Author*

control much longer sections of track, with the actual location of the train being indicated through track circuiting on a computer screen or wall-mounted diagram. In some of the power signal boxes, even a train passing right beside the box could be seen only on the diagram, not through glass!

From all of this it can be seen that the most significant change at Birdswood is that the lovely signal box has now gone. If only I could have been on hand before it was demolished, I may just have been able to recover a lever, a block instrument, the box diagram or a semaphore arm. Just where I would have kept such trophies or whether I could have obtained them by legal means is another matter. To think that such a lovely, well-cared-for signal box with all its happy associations was thoughtlessly reduced to a little pile of brick rubble, matchwood and scrap metal seems like a nightmare, and such a waste of good materials and equipment. But at least I have my memories.

While all this was going on, plans were formulated to close the public right of way that enabled local people to walk from Dutton village, over the railway by the signal box (as described elsewhere) and on to Aston, the hamlet on the far side of Birds Wood. Even when I frequented the box, the footpath was very little used and, by the time electrification came to the area, many people living in a remote place like Aston had a car. Yet it was not the infrequency of use that led to the path's closure, it was a matter of public safety.

Whereas in the 1950s someone using the path could easily tell if a train was coming by looking at the signals, by the noise it made and, if it was quite near, the vibration it caused, now it is not so clear. The signal arms are gone, the trains travel much faster, the motive power is quieter and an express could swiftly and almost silently appear on the scene, especially if a Driving Van Trailer was at the front and the locomotive at the rear of the train. Little wonder so many pedestrians have been killed by electric trains while using public rights of way over such fast lines. The high speed of today's trains is not generally appreciated.

Increasing line speed led BR managers to simplify track layouts at various places by removing what they considered to be unnecessary crossings and points. Birdswood was affected in several ways by this philosophy. First of all the trailing crossing from up main to down main – which can be seen just below the signal box in some of the photographs – was removed. Then the refuge siding was lifted, freeing up some space to allow the up and down main tracks of the West Coast Main Line to be slewed slightly eastwards, resulting in an easing of the curve and consequently permitting a slightly higher speed over that section of the tracks between the flyover and Dutton Tunnel.

Without doubt the most significant change of track layout in this area came with the repositioning of the so-called 'flying junction' formerly controlled by Weaver Junction signal box to a position just a few chains south of the Birdswood flyover. This meant that almost a mile of the Liverpool branch, which ran parallel to the down main track, could be lifted, with the resultant saving in track maintenance. It also meant that the speed limit of 55mph for down trains over the original long-bladed points at Weaver Junction could be removed for trains continuing along the West Coast Main Line, and increased to 80mph for trains taking the Liverpool branch. Yet another very good reason for extinguishing the public right of way across the tracks.

A layout change has also taken place on the down Liverpool track as it climbs at 1 in 101 towards Sutton Weaver. Immediately beside the Aston Lane road overbridge was a set of spring-loaded trap points designed to divert any runaway vehicles rolling back down the hill off the track and into the adjacent field out of harm's way. The steep gradient on this stretch of line would reduce a heavy freight train to walking pace as it breasted the summit, whereas even the 'Merseyside Express' with its long train of 16 or 17 bogies

would be slowed to something around 35mph. In the case of a freight train, the possibility of a broken coupling was a stark reality, especially if the locomotive stalled and a later attempt to restart on the hill was made. Any snatching could easily cause a coupling to part, so the wisdom of installing the runaway trap is obvious, especially when we remember that it is only relatively recently that freight wagons have been fitted with automatic brakes.

Another change that has taken place, but which would perhaps only be recognised by railway employees, is that the local platelaying gang no longer exists. The ganger (a kind of foreman) would give orders to his team of six men for whatever work needed to be done on the track and surrounding land. Leaving them to get on with whatever he had assigned them to do, he would then make his daily inspection of the length of track for which he was responsible. He would do this by walking from one end to the other, checking that nothing was amiss. He would look out particularly for any keys (holding the rails into the chairs on the sleepers) that may have been vibrated

These two views of the runaway trap near Sutton Weaver clearly show how any vehicle running away wrong line down the hill would be diverted away from the track and into the field, rather than rolling backwards to collide with any oncoming train. In the left-hand photograph we are looking downhill towards Birdswood, which lies around the corner beyond the far bridge, and where, incidentally, another set of trap points was installed on this track. In the heavy shadow of the overbridge there is a lockable lever that, when any wrong-line working is taking place, can be released in order to hold the points closed and thus allow traffic to proceed wrong line as far as Weaver Junction. I have never heard of any railway anecdotes relating to this equipment having been forced into use, but that is not to say that there were never any trucks that broke away from their train on this steep climb. *Both M. H. Walshaw*

loose by passing trains, and would deftly tap them back into place with the long-handled hammer he carried on his shoulder. He would also make a note of where any vegetation needed trimming, where ballast should be built up, or where rail, sleeper or fishplate needed to be replaced. Nowadays there are no local gangs, but teams from elsewhere arrive in a fleet of minibuses and vans to do what is required. In addition to their work on the tracks, members of the gang were expected to be on call in case of fog. When called out, they would go to the signal to which they had been assigned in order to replace any detonator that was exploded by a passing train. Of course on the modern railway such tasks are no longer necessary, as colour-light signals safely penetrate the fog, and various cab warning systems keep the drivers aware of the signal aspects. Even what is called cab-to-shore radio

enables drivers to keep in touch with the signalling centres many miles away.

Yet another major change has taken place in the area of the former Birdswood signal box. This came about as a direct result of the 'whisky and soda' accident mentioned in Chapter 12. Due to the fact that recovery teams had so much difficulty reaching the accident scene, it was decided to clear a track from the houses at the end of the canal tunnel, along the east side of the line towards Dutton Viaduct. Track maintenance teams were then able to gain access by road to the area where the junction points are located. Along with this came the need to build an electrical sub-station, which is almost opposite the point where Birdswood signal box stood. This building can be seen in the photograph taken from inside a 'Pendolino' train on page 90.

Away from Birdswood there have been

Perhaps the changes in this part of north Cheshire began earlier than might be imagined. From the railway viewpoint, the electrification programme inevitably brought about change, some evidence of which can be seen in this photograph of Runcorn station taken in May 1960. Modifications to the platforms are under way, which resulted in extending them southwards. But notice in the background a mammoth change taking place, which altered the whole skyline of the area. The

new Runcorn-Widnes road bridge is under construction and will eventually lead to the Transporter Bridge, seen just to the right of the station nameboard, becoming redundant; it was demolished shortly after the road bridge was commissioned. Add to this scene a forest of overhead line equipment masts and a 'Pendolino' in place of 'Black Five' No 45376 with its with Liverpool-Crewe stopping train, and we are right up to the start of the 21st century. *R. Stephens*

At Halton Junction the water tank and crane at the end of the goods loop from Yellow Bridge are about to become further casualties of the electrification programme. This scene looking down towards Runcorn shows the old and new signals. The signal box can be seen to the side of the right-hand signal, with the turn-out from the loop clearly visible. *R. Stephens*

significant alterations to the railway scene, perhaps the most apparent being the renaming of Norton station to become Runcorn East. Not only a change of name, but the platforms have been moved a couple of hundred yards westwards to more easily fit into the roadway pattern of the Runcorn New Town. At Runcorn itself, the station has been remodelled by considerably extending the platforms at the south end of the station, and replacing the original footbridge with a new one, which incorporates lifts for the disabled.

An unfortunate development as far as railways are concerned involves the link between Halton Junction and Frodsham Junction, which, until the building of the M56 and M53 motorways in the north of Cheshire, saw a regular passenger train service, principally between Chester and Liverpool Lime Street. However, due to more people using their cars to commute to the cities, train services were reduced, then withdrawn altogether. The direct result was that British Railways not only singled that section between Halton and Frodsham junctions, but redesignated it a freight-only route. Currently, however, a pressure group is fighting valiantly to get the line reopened to passenger traffic.

Perhaps a sign of the times is that not a single one of the several industrial estates or business parks that have sprung up during Runcorn's development have been rail-connected. In the case of some, it would

clearly not be viable to run even a single line to provide rail access, but some of the others are built within very easy striking distance of existing railways.

All the changes so far mentioned have been about the railway itself, yet these are not the only changes that have taken place between then and now. Just as an example, the village of Dutton itself has undergone such a transformation that it would no longer be recognisable to those who knew it in the 1950s. This has been due mainly to the expansion of Runcorn, the boundary of which now comes right up to the edge of the village of Dutton. Started in the 1960s by the Runcorn Development Corporation, the enlargement of what was originally a small town now encompasses the villages of Halton, Norton, Stockham, Astmoor, Weston, Weston Point, Clifton, Sutton Weaver and Preston Brook, and the railway stations at Halton and Preston Brook have been closed. As if to lay absolute claim to what was nothing more than open fields scattered around those villages, huge industrial estates and thousands of houses have been built as a permanent reminder that this is no longer open country with its small friendly village communities. One particular example may serve to illustrate the point: a huge warehouse-type modern building has been erected right on the very edge of Dutton village, and gives the impression of the town bully towering over

Above A Saturdays-only Blackpool Central to Euston express, W396, passes the switched-out signal box at Preston Brook and will soon pass Birdswood. Stanier Class 5 No 45015 pilots 'Jubilee' No 45705 *Seahorse*. Between the signal box and the train can be seen the Red Lion, where Joan and I occupied the top-floor flat after our wedding in February 1957. *J. A. Peden*

Right One of the factories built on the outskirts of Dutton village, as seen from the site of the former recovery hospital, where an estate of modern houses has been built. *Author*

the little village lad who has been terrified into submission. It appears to cast a shadow over the formerly open aspect of the village, and due to its immense size, does so literally when the sun shines.

Changes have also occurred in connection with two hospitals that were so much a part of village life in Dutton and which would have been well known to the railwaymen of the village. The former workhouse, standing at the crossroads of Northwich Road, Barkers Hollow Road and Higher Lane, surrounded on all sides by its 8-foot-high perimeter wall, so

dominated the village that the crossroads came to be known by all in the area as 'workhouse corner'. The tall, domed clock tower stood sentinel over everything within the walls, and could be seen for miles around, while the main gate opened onto a sweeping drive that led up to the main door. How formidable that must have seemed to prospective inmates in the days when it functioned as a workhouse, yet since the late 1940s it had been operating as a geriatric hospital, but with very little done to temper its foreboding appearance. As a natural casualty of cost-cutting in the National Health Service, this ageing complex of wards was sold off to a developer who, after demolishing the old Victorian buildings within the perimeter wall, built dwellings on the site and rather fortuitously kept most of the wall.

The other hospital at Dutton was built to accommodate fever sufferers and was duly named an isolation hospital, but from the 1950s it came to be used as a recovery hospital. It was located in the fork between the West Coast Main Line heading north to Warrington and the branch bearing west towards Runcorn and Liverpool. It has to be said that part of the railway noise would have been absorbed by the many trees on the site, some of which had been felled when the hospital was built. Even so, it must have been pretty obvious to patients that they were very close to a railway. It must have been frustrating for any who were rail enthusiasts, because they would have heard the noises and felt the vibrations of passing trains, but would not have been able to see them unless they went to the perimeter fence. This hospital was also closed and demolished, and eventually the site was sold off and redeveloped for housing. I was quite surprised just how far this triangle of wooded land has been developed, because the present housing scheme penetrates further towards the point where Birdswood signal box was located than did the hospital and its outbuildings. In fact, the most westerly of the new houses is merely 80 metres or so from where the signal box stood, being separated only by the now-typical railway fence of galvanised angle-iron palings. It backs onto the Warrington line, presenting its occupants with a grandstand view of the passing trains, if indeed they have any railway interest.

The only licensed premises in Dutton village, referred to in these pages as the Talbot Arms, has itself been the subject of change with the passing of time. It was formerly known as the Tunnel Top, due to being built almost exactly above the halfway point of the tunnel carrying the Trent & Mersey Canal from Birdswood to Preston Brook. However, just after the Second World War its name was changed by the owning brewery to the Talbot Arms, reflecting an acknowledgement of a very influential land-owning family in the parish, and naturally the pub sign proudly displayed the Talbot coat-of-arms. Whether due to a decline in the Talbot family influence or for other reasons, the name has recently reverted to the Tunnel Top, which, after all, more precisely fits the circumstances. The many railwaymen who – going off duty after a long shift at work – would have slaked their thirst at that hostelry on their way home would undoubtedly have approved, and I know that many of them always referred to it as the Tunnel Top, whatever it was officially named.

All the changes mentioned in this chapter have taken place since the railway was electrified and were without doubt the natural consequences of local development coupled with the changing lifestyles of the village personalities. They should – to a lesser or greater extent – have been expected but, however they have occurred and for whatever reasons, they consigned to the history books a way of life that had hitherto been followed for decades. The clock cannot be turned back, and the village of Dutton will never be the same again. So you, the reader, must decide for yourself if matters have improved or deteriorated.

As for me, I am more than grateful to be able to nurture the catalogue of happy memories of how things were and to have shared them with you through these pages.

APPENDIX 1
SCHEDULE OF TRAINS PASSING BIRDSWOOD, SPRING 1953

u	up train	TThO	Tuesdays and Thursdays only
d	down train	SO	Saturday only
MO	Monday only	SX	except Saturday
MOQ	Monday only if required	Q	runs as required
MX	except Monday		

Time and direction		No	Train details	Class	Days	Remarks
pm						
10 00	d		9.40pm Crewe-Liverpool Lime St	B	SX	
10 06	u		9.05pm Edge Hill-Crewe	E	SX	
10 08	u	38	12.35pm Perth-Willesden Jn	A	MO	
10 20	d		9.50pm Crewe-Bamfurlong	H	SX	
10 22	u		9.45pm Warrington-Crewe	H	SX	
10 29	u	304	9.50pm Liverpool Lime St-Euston	A	SX	
10 31	d	151	7.20pm Euston-Inverness	A	SX	
10 35	u	418	8.30pm Blackpool North-Crewe	A	MFO	
10 44	d	151	7.20pm Euston-Inverness	A	SX	
10 46	u	400	8.30pm Kendal-Euston	A	SX	
10 47	u		6.40pm Blackpool-Crewe	D	SX	
10 51	d	149	7.25pm Euston-Perth	F	SXQ	
10 55	d		10.25pm Crewe-Warrington	H	FSX	
11 05	d	307	10.50pm Crewe-Perth	A	SXQ	
11 10	u	142	10.10pm Liverpool Lime St-Crewe	A		
11 10	d		10.40pm Crewe-Warrington	H	SX	
11 15	d		10.45pm Crewe-Preston Ribble Sdg	F	MX	
11 15	u	154	5.30pm Glasgow St Enoch-Plymouth	A	FO	
11 18	u		9.50pm Edge Hill-Northampton	E	MSX	
11 25	u	326	9.25pm Blackpool Central-Euston	A	FO	
11 25	u	392	12.10pm Aberdeen-Broad St	C	FSX	
11 25	d	153	7.30pm Euston-Perth	A		
11 30	d		7.45pm Curzon St-Edge Hill	D	SX	
11 31	u		10.15pm Edge Hill-Nottingham	E	SX	
11 35	d		10.45pm Alsager Jn-Speke Sdg	J		
11 39	d	155	7.55pm Euston-Stranraer Harbour	A	SX	'The Northern Irishman'
11 41	u		10.15pm Edge Hill-Northampton	E	SX	
11 42	u	326	9.35pm Blackpool Central-Euston	A		
11 48	u	370	8.30pm Windermere-Euston	A		
am						
12 10	u	148	6.25pm Glasgow Central-Euston	A		
12 14	u		10.55pm Edge Hill-Crewe	H	MSX	
12 15	d	157	8.30pm Euston-Glasgow Central	A		
12 15	u		5.15pm Carlisle-Crewe	D	SX	
12 16	u	140	11.35pm Liverpool Lime St-Euston	A	MO	
12 20	d		7.35pm Camden-Edge Hill	C	SX	

Time and direction		No	Train details	Class	Days	Remarks
12 26	u	146	5.40pm Glasgow Central-Euston	A	MX	
12 30	d	169	9.10pm Euston-Glasgow Central	A		
12 31	u	158	11.45pm Liverpool Lime St-Crewe	A	MX	
12 33	u	146	5.45pm Glasgow Central-Euston	A	MO	
12 34	d	385	12.15am Crewe-Preston	C	MX	
12 38	d	175	9.17pm Euston-Glasgow St Enoch	A	MOQ	
12 39	u	158	11.45pm Liverpool Lime St-Crewe	A	MO	
12 45	d	205	12.00pm Penzance-Liverpool Lime St	A		
12 50	u		5.30pm Carlisle-Crewe	H		
12 55	d		12.35am Crewe-Carlisle	A	FMX	
12 58	u	152	12.10am Liverpool Lime St-Euston	A		
12 58	u		12.12am Warrington-Nuneaton	F	MX	
1 00	d	267	12.45am Crewe-Liverpool Lime St	A	MO	
1 02	u		6.05pm Carlisle-Crewe	H	MO	
1 04	u		2.50pm Carlisle-Crewe	F	MX	
1 05	d	291	10.50pm Birmingham-Glasgow Central	A	Q	
1 07	u		12.33am Warrington-Nuneaton	F	MX	
1 15	d		1.00am Crewe-Edge Hill	E	MX	
1 17	u		12.33am Warrington-Coventry	F		
1 20	d	299	11.10pm Birmingham-Glasgow Central	A		
1 27	u	362	7.20pm Law Jn-Birmingham	C	MX	
1 30	d		12.55am Crewe-Walton Old Jn	H		
1 40	d	171	9.25pm Euston-Glasgow Central	A		
1 46	u	182	1.10am Liverpool Lime St-Crewe	C	MX	
1 51	u		12.40am Edge Hill-Stoke	F	MSX	
1 55	d		8.40pm Nottingham-Edge Hill	E	MX	
1 55	u		10.45pm Carnforth-Crewe	H	MO	
2 05	d		1.35am Crewe-Garston Speke Sdg	H	MO	
2 05	d		8.40pm Coventry-Edge Hill	D	SX	
2 06	u		11.25pm Burn Naze-Willesden HL	F	TThO	
2 06	u		1.35am Warrington-Nuneaton	F	MO	
2 08	d		8.50pm Camden-Carnforth	C	MX	
2 17	u	156	10.15pm Carlisle-Broad St	C	MO	
2 20	d	195	10.52pm Euston-Perth	A	SX	
2 20	u		1.10am Edge Hill-Crewe	F	MX	
2 25	d	231	2.10am Crewe-Liverpool Lime St	B	MX	
2 25	d		9.00pm Camden-Preston	D	MX	
2 30	d		1.05am Harlescott Sdg-Carlisle	E	MO	
2 31	d	193	2.16am Crewe-Windermere	A	MO	
2 33	d	193	11.05pm Euston-Windermere	A	SX	
2 40	d	183	11.15pm Euston-Blackpool North	A	MO	
2 40	d		2.20am Crewe-Springs Branch	E	MO	
2 45	u		1.40am Edge Hill-Curzon St	F	MX	
2 45	d		10.25pm Aston-Edge Hill	E	MX	
2 50	d	21	11.40pm Euston-Carlisle	A	SX	
2 50	d	231	2.35am Crewe-Liverpool Lime St	B	MO	
2 56	u		1.57am Edge Hill-Curzon St	F	MO	
3 00	u		2.00am Speke Sdg-Crewe	H	MX	
3 05	d	21	11.40pm Euston-Glasgow Central	A	SO	
3 07	u	10	9.25pm Glasgow Central-Euston	A		
3 10	d		11.14pm Curzon St-Preston	E	MX	
3 17	d	3	10.00pm Euston-Preston	A	SX	
3 20	d		12.30am Harlescott Sdg-Carlisle	F	MO	

Time and direction		No	Train details	Class	Days	Remarks
3 20	d	167	3.05am Crewe-Preston	C	MO	
3 25	u	12	8.25pm Perth-Euston	A		
3 31	d	475	12.02am Birmingham-Carlisle	C	MX	
3 35	u	6	10.10pm Glasgow Central-Euston	A		
3 38	u	380	7.40pm Carlisle-Rugby	C	MX	
3 43	d	3	10.00pm Broad St-Preston	C	SX	
3 50	d	213	12.30am Euston-Liverpool Lime St	A		
3 55	u	14	8.55pm Perth-Euston	A	MO	
3 55	d		10.00pm Camden-Warrington	D	MX	
3 55	u	14	4.45pm Inverness-Euston	A	TO	
4 00	d		3.30am Crewe-Bamfurlong	H	MO	
4 05	u	224	10.25pm Glasgow Central-Euston	A		
4 08	u		3.00am Bamfurlong-Bushbury	E	MO	
4 10	u		9.05pm Carlisle-Crewe	F	MX	
4 25	d		2.05am Harlescott Sdg-Bamfurlong	H	MO	
4 25	d		2.15am Bescot-Carlisle Kingmoor	D	MX	
4 27	u	68	10.00pm Stranraer Harbour-Euston	A	MX	'The Northern Irishman'
4 37	u	16	5.35pm Inverness-Euston	A	MX	
4 45	u	18	11.15pm Glasgow Central-Birmingham	A		
4 50	d		4.20am Crewe-Edge Hill	F	MO	
4 55	u		9.10pm Carlisle-Crewe	H	MO	
4 57	u		4.23 Perth-Maiden Lane	D	WThFO	
5 00	d		4.30am Crewe-Edge Hill	F	MO	
5 00	d		9.55pm Willesden-Carlisle	C	MX	
5 01	u		3.30am Edge Hill-Alsager Jn	F	MX	
5 05	d		2.43am Harlescott Sdg-Edge Hill	H	MX	
5 10	d		10.05pm Willesden-Carlisle	D	MX	
5 15	d		4.45am Crewe-Runcorn	H	MO	
5 15	d	209	5.00am Crewe-Liverpool Lime St	C	MX	
5 15	u		4.15am Speke Sdg-Crewe	H	MO	
5 15	u		11.50pm Carnforth-Crewe	H	MX	
5 17	u		4.15am Garston-Crewe	H	MO	
5 20	d		2.48am Armington Sdg-Edge Hill	E	MO	
5 25	d		3.15am Bescot-Carlisle London Rd	E	SX	
5 35	u		5.00am Warrington-Crewe	H	MX	
5 35	d	215	12.05am Cardiff-Liverpool Lime St	A	MO	
5 35	d		5.15am Crewe-Warrington	D	WFO	
5 35	d		12.20am Camden-Carlisle	D	MX	
5 38	d		2.43 Harlescott Sdg-Edge Hill	H	MO	
5 41	d	215	12.05am Cardiff-Liverpool Lime St	A	MX	
5 48	u		4.20am Edge Hill-Crewe	H	MO	
6 00	d	31	5.45am Crewe-Morecambe Prom	C	MX	
6 00	d		5.30am Crewe-Runcorn	H	MO	
6 05	d		5.35am Crewe-Garston Speke Sdg	H	MX	
6 10	u		5.15am Edge Hill-Sudbury Jn	E	MX	
6 20	d		5.50am Crewe-Walton Old Jn	H	MX	
6 20	d		6.00am Crewe-Warrington	B		
6 25	u		3.22am Carnforth-Bushbury	H	SX	
6 25	d		5.55am Crewe-Walton Old Jn	H	MO	
6 37	d		6.07am Crewe-Walton Old Jn	H	MSX	
6 45	d		11.20pm Kirkby-Garston Speke Sdg	J	MSX	
6 46	u		5.00am Warrington-Crewe	H	MO	
6 55	d		6.15am Crewe-Edge Hill	H	MX	

Time and direction		No	Train details	Class	Days	Remarks
7 08	d		6.10am Stoke-Liverpool Lime St	B		
7 12	d		6.42am Crewe-Bamfurlong	H	MO	
7 13	u		5.30am Preston-Crewe	B		
7 20	d		3.30am Bescot-Warrington	H	MO	
7 20	d		5.20am Harlescott Sdg-Bamfurlong	H	MSX	
7 28	u	372	12.1am Glasgow Central-Euston	C	MX	
7 40	u	390	4.28am Carlisle-Crewe	C	MX	
7 53	d		7.23am Crewe-Aintree	F	SX	
7 55	d		4.05am Washwood Heath-Aintree	F	SX	
8 00	u		3.10am Carlisle-Crewe	D		
8 02	d		7.42am Crewe-Liverpool Lime St	B		
8 10	d		7.40am Crewe-Carlisle London Rd	H	SX	
8 16	u	32	6.30am Heysham-Euston	A		'The Ulster Express'
8 29	u	272	6.30am Morecambe-Crewe	A		
8 30	d		2.20am Northampton-Walton Old Jn	H	MO	
8 30	d		8.00am Crewe-Warrington	H	MSX	
8 35	u		4.15am Carnforth-Crewe	H	SX	
8 47	u	34	8.00am Liverpool Lime St-Birmingham	A		
8 50	d		4.40am Harlescott Sdg-Carlisle	E	SX	
8 50	d		2.45am Northampton-Walton Old Jn	H	MSX	
8 55	u	36	8.20am Liverpool Lime St-Euston	A		
9 05	d		6.35am Harlescott Sdg-Bamfurlong	H	MSX	
9 08	d	223	8.00am Stoke-Liverpool Lime St	B		
9 20	u		8.50am Runcorn-Crewe South Shed	G	MO	
9 21	d		3.50am Northampton-Aintree	F	MSX	
9 30	d		9.10am Crewe-Liverpool Lime St	B		
9 30	u		8.20am Edge Hill-Nuneaton	F	MSX	
9 40	u	26	7.25am Heysham-Crewe	A		
9 40	d	27	9.25am Crewe-Perth	A	SX	
9 45	d		9.10am Crewe-Runcorn	H	SX	
9 49	u	208	9.05am Liverpool Lime St-Plymouth	A	SX	
9 54	u	296	8.00am Blackpool Central-Euston	A	SX	
9 55	d	389	9.40am Crewe-Blackpool North	A	MFO	
10 07	d	225	8.30am Birmingham-Liverpool Lime St	A	SX	
10 15	u		9.20am Edge Hill-Crewe	E	MSX	
10 17	d		9.27am Alsager-Garston Speke Sdg	J	SX	
10 23	u		4.05am Carlisle-Sudbury Jn	D	SX	
10 40	u	54	10.10am Liverpool Lime St-Euston	A		'The Merseyside Express'
10 46	u	62	10.15am Liverpool Lime St-Crewe	A	SX	
10 54	u		10.00am Runcorn-Wichnor Jn	J	MO	
11 00	d	229	9.15am Birmingham-Liverpool Lime St	A		
11 03	d		10.40am Crewe-Carlisle	D	SX	
11 19	u		10.50am Runcorn-Alsager Jn	F	SX	
11 20	d	33	6.40am Euston-Windermere	A		
11 22	d		7.30am Three Spires Jn-Aintree	F	MO	
11 25	u	274	6.05am Carlisle-Crewe	A		
11 29	d	33	6.40am Euston-Windermere	A		
11 41	u	112	11.10am Liverpool Lime St-Euston	A		
11 42	d		9.30am Sideway-Garston Speke Sdg	J	SX	
11 50	d		11.20am Crewe-Warrington	H	SX	
11 55	d		11.25am Crewe-Walton Old Jn	H	SX	
11 55	u	330	10.00am Blackpool Central-Euston	A	SX	
11 59	d	39	8.30am Euston-Liverpool Lime St	A		

Time and direction		No	Train details	Class	Days	Remarks
pm						
12 10	d		6.55am Chaddesden-Runcorn	J	MSX	
12 14	u		10.55am Edge Hill-Crewe	H	SX	
12 20	u		11.36am Garston-Crewe	D	SX	
12 23	d	43	12.8pm Crewe-Blackpool Central	A		
12 30	d		12.00pm Crewe-Garston Speke Sdg	H	MSX	
12 36	u	74	8.20am Carlisle-Euston	A		
12 38	d		12.18pm Crewe-Liverpool Lime St	A		
12 44	u	84	11.40am Liverpool Lime St-Rugby Mid	A		
12 45	d	367	12.30pm Crewe-Carlisle	C	SX	
12 50	u		5.30am Carlisle-Crewe	H	SX	
12 55	d	67	11.15am Birmingham-Glasgow Central	A		
12 55	u		11.55am Bamfurlong-Crewe	F	SX	
1 10	d	63	10.00am Euston-Glasgow Central	A		'The Royal Scot'
1 10	u		5.15am Carlisle-Bushbury	E		
1 12	u		11.50am Edge Hill-Shrewsbury	F	SX	
1 20	u		12.10pm Edge Hill-Bushbury	F	SX	
1 20	d		9.30am Bescot-Warrington	F	MSX	
1 30	u		12.55pm Warrington-Crewe	H	MSX	
1 30	d	57	10.08am Euston-Glasgow Central	A		
1 40	u		12.40pm Garston-Crewe	D	SX	
1 40	u		6.50am Carlisle-Crewe	H	SX	
1 43	d	71	10.30am Euston-Liverpool Lime St	A		'The Manxman'
1 48	d	65	10.20am Euston-Perth	A		
2 00	u	86	8.35am Workington-Euston	A	SX	'The Lakes Express'
2 09	d	251	10.40am Euston-Carlisle	A		
2 12	u		1.15pm Edge Hill-Willesden	D	FSO	
2 14	u		1.00pm Edge Hill-Crewe	H	SX	
2 20	d		1.50pm Crewe-Edge Hill	H	SX	
2 20	d		2.00pm Crewe-Liverpool Lime St	B		
2 30	u	92	2.00pm Liverpool Lime St-Euston	A		'The Manxman'
2 33	d	77	10.50am Euston-Blackpool Central	A	SX	
2 35	u		1.30pm Edge Hill-Willesden HL	D	SX	
2 38	u		1.25pm Runcorn-Alsager	F	SX	
2 39	u	106	8.35am Stirling-Birmingham	A	MFSO	
2 40	d	77	10.50am Euston-Blackpool Central	A	SO	
2 40	u	98	9.30am Glasgow Central-Birmingham	A		
2 53	u	96	10.00am Glasgow Central-Euston	A		'The Royal Scot'
2 55	d		2.25pm Crewe-Bamfurlong	H		
3 02	u		2.00pm Edge Hill-Nuneaton	F	SX	
3 10	u		2.10pm Edge Hill-Nuneaton	E	SX	
3 15	u		2.10pm Garston-Crewe	D	SX	
3 19	d	121	11.55am Euston-Workington	A	MFSO	'The Lakes Express'
3 27	d	179	3.12pm Crewe-Workington	A	SX	
3 40	u	234	3.00pm Liverpool Lime St-Cardiff	A	SX	
3 43	d	83	12.30pm Euston-Liverpool Lime St	A		'The Red Rose'
3 50	d	255	1.45pm Birmingham-Liverpool Lime St	A	SX	
3 51	u	110	8.55am Perth-Euston	A	MFSO	
4 00	u		2.54pm Garston-Crewe	D	SX	
4 03	d	343	3.48pm Crewe-Liverpool Lime St	S	SX	
4 03	u	254	10.50am Workington-Euston	A	MFO	
4 08	u	356	8.35am Carlisle-Crewe	C	SX	
4 23	u		3.15pm Edge Hill-Bushbury	H	SX	

Time and direction		No	Train details	Class	Days	Remarks
4 36	u	266	1.30pm Barrow-Euston	A		
4 39	d	97	1.15pm Euston-Glasgow Central	A		'The Mid-day Scot'
4 41	u	114	4.10pm Liverpool Lime St-Euston	A		
4 48	d	99	4.33pm Crewe-Blackpool Central	A	FOQ	
4 50	u		3.05pm Speke Jn-Alsager	F	SX	
4 50	d		4.30pm Crewe-Carlisle Kingmoor	D		
4 55	d	93	1.30pm Euston-Blackpool Central	A		
5 05	u	162	4.17pm Liverpool Lime St-Crewe	A		
5 10	u		3.50pm Garston-Crewe	D	SX	
5 15	d	263	8.45am Plymouth-Liverpool Lime St	A		
5 25	d		5.05pm Crewe-Liverpool Lime St	B		
5 44	u		5.20pm Warrington-Crewe	B		
5 45	d	113	2.22pm Euston-Liverpool Lime St	A	FSO	
5 47	d		5.15pm Crewe-Garston Speke Sdg	H	SX	
5 55	u	122	5.25pm Liverpool Lime St-Euston	A		'The Red Rose'
6 06	d	115	2.30pm Euston-Liverpool Lime St	A		
6 10	u		5.05pm Garston-Crewe	D	SX	
6 15	d	397	6.00pm Crewe-Carlisle	A		
6 20	u		4.20pm Edge Hill-Crewe	H	SX	
6 34	d		2.40pm Camden-Glasgow Buchanan St	C	SX	
6 40	u	126	1.30pm Glasgow Central-Euston	A		'The Mid-day Scot'
6 45	u		5.40pm Liverpool Lime St-Crewe	B		
6 45	d	383	7.40am Penzance-Liverpool Lime St	A	SX	
6 52	d	73	6.37pm Crewe-Carlisle	C		
7 00	u		6.40pm Runcorn-Crewe	F	SX	
7 11	d		2.40pm Camden-Glasgow Buchanan St	C	SO	
7 15	u	136	5.05pm Blackpool Central-Euston	A		
7 30	u		3.50pm Carlisle-Broad St	C	TWThO	
7 33	d	269	4.15pm Euston-Liverpool Lime St	A	FO	
7 40	u		6.25pm Edge Hill-Crewe	F		
7 45	d		7.25pm Crewe-Carlisle	E	SX	
7 45	u	250	7.05pm Liverpool Lime St-Birmingham	A	SX	
7 52	d	85	4.30pm Euston-Liverpool Lime St	A		
7 54	u		5.30pm Carnforth-Willesden	C	MX	
8 00	u		7.00pm Garston-Crewe	D	SX	
8 03	d	279	6.05pm Birmingham-Liverpool Lime St	A		
8 12	d	247	4.47pm Euston-Heysham	A	FO	'The Ulster Express'
8 19	d	141	4.55pm Euston-Heysham	A	FSX	'The Ulster Express'
8 21	u		7.20pm Liverpool Lime St-Crewe	B		
8 33	u		7.32pm Garston-Willesden HL	D	SX	
8 36	d	159	5.05pm Euston-Blackpool Central	A		
8 42	d	447	8.27pm Crewe-Preston	S	SX	
8 44	u		4.42pm Carlisle-Willesden HL	C	SX	
9 05	d	285	10.05am Penzance-Liverpool Lime St	A	SX	
9 19	u		8.30pm Edge Hill-Camden	D	SX	
9 20	d	137	6.07pm Euston-Liverpool Lime St	A		'The Merseyside Express'
9 30	d		9.00pm Crewe-Edge Hill	H		
9 35	d		9.15pm Crewe-Carnforth	F	FSX	
9 42	d	131	6.20pm Euston-Preston	A	SX	
9 43	u		9.10pm Warrington-Camden	D	SX	
9 47	u		6.40pm Blackpool-Crewe	D	SX	
9 48	u		8.50pm Edge Hill-Curzon St	E	SX	

APPENDIX 2
SIGNALLING DIAGRAMS

Based upon *BR Layout Plans of the 1950s*, from the John Swift collection, Vols 9 and 10, published by the Signalling Record Society.

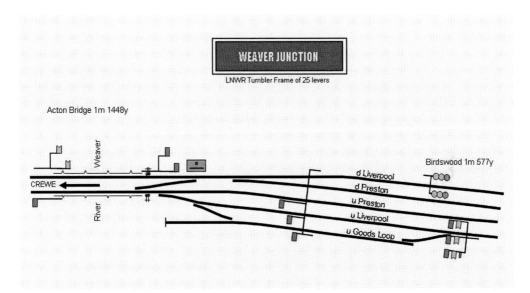

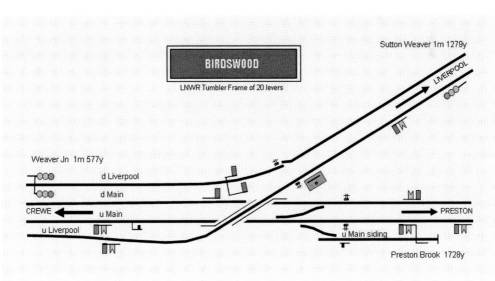

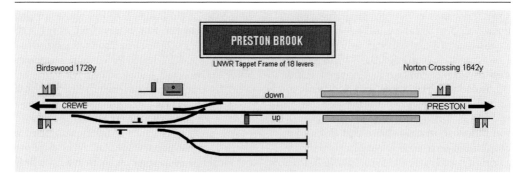

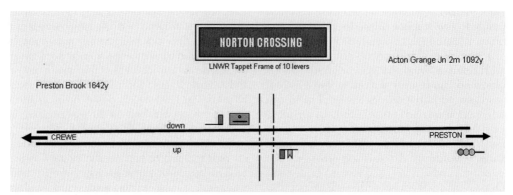

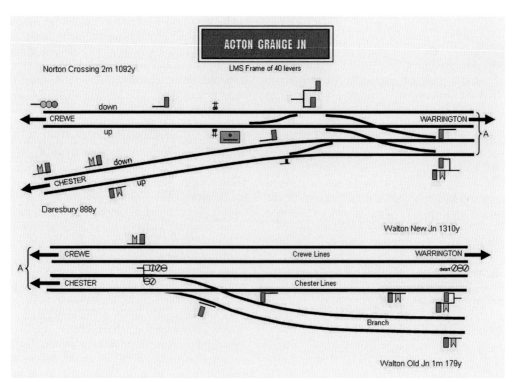

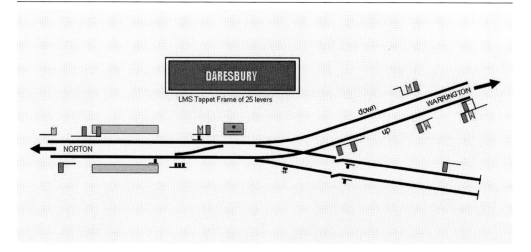

DARESBURY

LMS Tappet Frame of 25 levers

NORTON

down

up

WARRINGTON

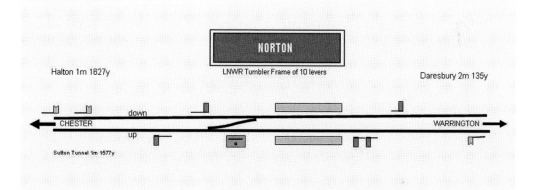

NORTON

LNWR Tumbler Frame of 10 levers

Halton 1m 1627y

Daresbury 2m 135y

down

CHESTER

up

WARRINGTON

Sutton Tunnel 1m 1577y

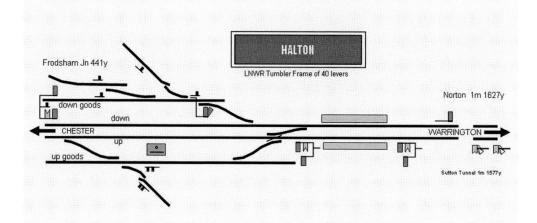

HALTON

LNWR Tumbler Frame of 40 levers

Frodsham Jn 441y

down goods

down

CHESTER

up

up goods

Norton 1m 1627y

WARRINGTON

Sutton Tunnel 1m 1577y

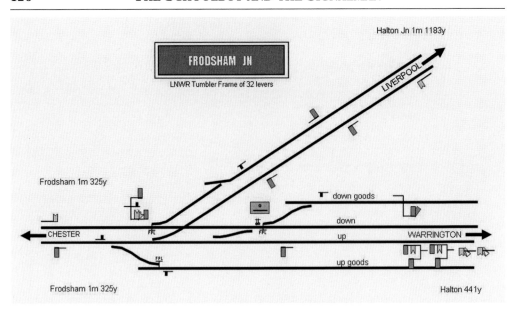

FRODSHAM JN

LNWR Tumbler Frame of 32 levers

Halton Jn 1m 1183y

LIVERPOOL

Frodsham 1m 325y

down goods

down

CHESTER

up

WARRINGTON

up goods

Frodsham 1m 325y

Halton 441y

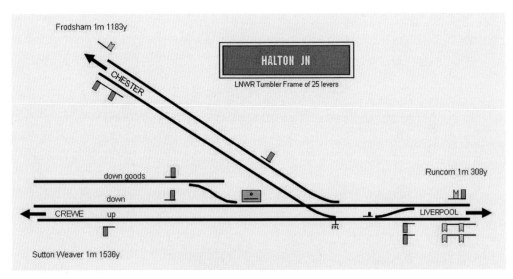

Frodsham 1m 1183y

HALTON JN

LNWR Tumbler Frame of 25 levers

CHESTER

Runcorn 1m 308y

down goods

down

CREWE

up

LIVERPOOL

Sutton Weaver 1m 1536y

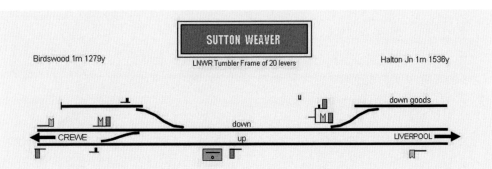

SUTTON WEAVER

LNWR Tumbler Frame of 20 levers

Birdswood 1m 1279y

Halton Jn 1m 1536y

down goods

down

CREWE

up

LIVERPOOL

APPENDIX 3
CODE OF BELL SIGNALS

CODE OF BELL SIGNALS to be used in describing trains in No. I Column of the Train Register Book.

Diagram showing classification, Headcodes and corresponding Bell Signals.

Note.—In addition to inserting the Bell Signal, Signalmen should enter any further information which may be necessary to identify the particular train, such as "starting point," "starting time," "name of train," "time train is due," &c.

Bell Signal	Description
4.	Express Passenger Train, Newspaper Train, or Break-down Van Train, or Snow Plough, going to clear the line, or Light Engine going to assist disabled train. Officers' Special Train not requiring to stop in section.
4—I—3.	Express Diesel Car.
3—I.	Ordinary Passenger Train, Mixed Train, or Break-down Van Train NOT going to clear the line, or loaded Rail Motor Train. ‡
I—3.	† Branch Passenger Train.
5—I—3.	Ordinary Passenger Diesel or Parcels Diesel Car.
I—3—I.	Parcels, Fish, Fruit, Horse, Livestock, Meat, Milk, Pigeon, or Perishable Train composed entirely of vehicles conforming to coaching stock requirements.
3—I—I.	Express Freight, Livestock, Perishable or Ballast Train pipe fitted throughout with the automatic brake operative on not less than half of the vehicles.
2—2—I.	Empty Coaching Stock Train (not specially authorised to carry "A" headcode), or Empty Rail Motor Train. ‡
5.	Express Freight, Livestock, Perishable or Ballast Train, partly fitted with the automatic brake operative on not less than one-third of the vehicles
I—2—2.	Express Freight, Livestock, Perishable or Ballast Train partly fitted with not less than four braked vehicles connected by vacuum pipe to the engine.
I—2—2.	Express Freight, Livestock, Perishable or Ballast Train with a limited load of vehicles NOT fitted with continuous brake.
3—2.	Express Freight, Livestock, Perishable or Ballast Train NOT fitted with continuous brake.
2—3.	Light Engine, or Light Engines coupled.
I—I—3.	Engine with not more than two brake vans.
I—4.	Through Freight or Ballast Train not running under Class "C," "D," "E" or "F" headcode.
4—I.	Mineral or Empty Wagon Train.
3.	Freight, Mineral or Ballast Train stopping at intermediate stations.
I—2.	† Branch Freight Train.
2—2—3.	Freight, Ballast, or Officers' Special Train requiring to stop in section.
2—6—2.	Train conveying out of gauge or exceptional load.
2—I—2.	Trolley requiring to go into or pass through Tunnel.

Any other specially authorised bell signals should also be inserted as required in column I.

† To be used only where authorised.
‡ The term "rail motor train" includes "auto train."

INDEX